First World War
and Army of Occupation
War Diary
France, Belgium and Germany

40 DIVISION
Divisional Troops
Alexandra, Princess of Wales's Own (Yorkshire Regiment)
12th Battalion Pioneers
27 May 1916 - 28 June 1918

WO95/2601/3

The Naval & Military Press Ltd
www.nmarchive.com
Published in association with The National Archives

Published by

The Naval & Military Press Ltd

Unit 10 Ridgewood Industrial Park,

Uckfield, East Sussex,

TN22 5QE England

Tel: +44 (0) 1825 749494

www.naval-military-press.com

www.nmarchive.com

This diary has been reprinted in facsimile from the original. Any imperfections are inevitably reproduced and the quality may fall short of modern type and cartographic standards.

© **Crown Copyright**
Images reproduced by permission of The National Archives, London, England, 2015.

Contents

Document type	Place/Title	Date From	Date To
Heading	WO95/260/3		
Heading	12th Bn Yorkshire Regt (Pioneers) Jun 1916-Jun 1918		
Miscellaneous	12th Yorkshire Regiment (Teeside Pioneers)		
Miscellaneous	O.C. 12th York Regt (Pioneers)	01/07/1916	01/07/1916
War Diary	Pirbright	27/05/1916	27/05/1916
War Diary	Southampton	01/06/1916	01/06/1916
War Diary	Havre	02/06/1916	03/06/1916
War Diary	Lillers	04/06/1916	04/06/1916
War Diary	Rely	04/06/1916	09/06/1916
War Diary	Fouquieres	10/06/1916	13/06/1916
War Diary	Mazingarbe	14/06/1916	30/06/1916
Heading	D.A.G. 3rd Echelon		
War Diary	Houchin	01/07/1916	02/07/1916
War Diary	South Maroc	03/07/1916	31/07/1916
Miscellaneous	O.C. 12th York Regt. To D.A.G. 3rd Echelon	01/09/1916	01/09/1916
War Diary	South Maroc	01/08/1916	31/08/1916
Miscellaneous	D.A.G., 3rd Echelon	01/10/1916	01/10/1916
War Diary	Loos	01/09/1916	30/09/1916
Miscellaneous	D.A.G. 3rd Echelon	01/11/1916	01/11/1916
War Diary	Loos	01/10/1916	27/10/1916
War Diary	Loos & Mazingarbe	28/10/1916	28/10/1916
War Diary	Mazingarbe	29/10/1916	29/10/1916
War Diary	Mazingarbe & Brury	30/10/1916	30/10/1916
War Diary	Brury & Marquay	31/10/1916	31/10/1916
Operation(al) Order(s)	Operation Order No 1 by Lieut Colonel A.W. Becker Commdg Loos Defences	04/10/1916	04/10/1916
Heading	Officer i/c Records	01/12/1916	01/12/1916
War Diary	Marqury	01/11/1916	01/11/1916
War Diary	Marqury & Moncheaux	02/11/1916	02/11/1916
War Diary	Moncheaux	03/11/1916	03/11/1916
War Diary	Moncheaux & Bonnieres & Boovoir	04/11/1916	04/11/1916
War Diary	Bonnieres & Bouvoir Outre Bois	05/11/1916	05/11/1916
War Diary	Outre Bois	06/11/1916	08/11/1916
War Diary	Outre Bois & Montigny	09/11/1916	09/11/1916
War Diary	Montigny	10/11/1916	10/11/1916
War Diary	Montigny & Montre Let	11/11/1916	11/11/1916
War Diary	Montrelet & Beauval	12/11/1916	12/11/1916
War Diary	Beauval & Doullens	13/11/1916	13/11/1916
War Diary	Doullens & Bayencourt	14/11/1916	14/11/1916
War Diary	Bayencourt	15/11/1916	19/11/1916
War Diary	Bayencourt & Halloy.	20/11/1916	20/11/1916
War Diary	Halloy	21/11/1916	21/11/1916
War Diary	Halloy & Authieule	22/11/1916	22/11/1916
War Diary	Authieule & Berneuil	23/11/1916	23/11/1916
War Diary	Bernguil & Ailly-Le Haut-Clocher	24/11/1916	24/11/1916
War Diary	Ailly-Le-Haut-Clocher	25/11/1916	30/11/1916
Miscellaneous	D.A.G. 3rd Echelon	01/01/1917	01/01/1917
War Diary	Ailly-Le-Haut-Clocher	01/12/1916	09/12/1916
War Diary	Briey	10/12/1916	10/12/1916
War Diary	Maurepas	11/12/1916	24/12/1916

Type	Location	From	To
War Diary	Near-Maurepas B. 20. a. 1.8. (Albert Sheet)	25/12/1916	31/12/1916
War Diary	Nr Maurepas	01/01/1917	26/01/1917
War Diary	Camp 14 Camp 23	27/01/1917	01/02/1917
War Diary	Camp 14 & Nissen huts Nr Curlu	02/02/1917	10/02/1917
War Diary	Nissen huts Nr Curlu And Maurepas Ravine	11/02/1917	28/02/1917
Miscellaneous	D.A.G. Base.	01/04/1917	01/04/1917
War Diary	Nissen huts Nr Curlu & Maurepas Ravine	01/03/1917	06/03/1917
War Diary	Nr Hem-Curlu Road about 1 mile from Curlu	07/03/1917	21/03/1917
War Diary	Berlin Valley (just East of Clery)	22/03/1917	24/03/1917
War Diary	Andover Place	25/03/1917	31/03/1917
Miscellaneous	D.A.G. Base		
War Diary	Andover Place	01/04/1917	06/04/1917
War Diary	Riverside Wood	07/04/1917	28/04/1917
War Diary	V. 11.G. Nr Fins	29/04/1917	30/04/1917
Miscellaneous	C.R.E 40th Division.	04/04/1917	04/04/1917
Miscellaneous	D.A.G., Base. Herewith War Diary for the month of May, 1917		
War Diary	Nr Fins (V. 11.b)	01/05/1917	31/05/1917
Miscellaneous	D.A.G., Base Herewith War Diary for the month of June, 1917		
War Diary	Nr Fins (V. 11.b)	01/06/1917	25/06/1917
War Diary	W.3.C.5.7.	26/06/1917	30/06/1917
Miscellaneous	D.A.G., Base		
War Diary	W. 3. C. 5.7.	01/07/1917	31/07/1917
Miscellaneous	D.A.G. 3rd Echelon.		
War Diary	W 3.C. 5.7	01/08/1917	30/09/1917
Miscellaneous	D.A.G., Base.		
War Diary	W.3.C.5.7.	01/10/1917	18/10/1917
War Diary	Peronne Lacoochie	19/10/1917	29/10/1917
War Diary	Moislains	30/10/1917	19/11/1917
War Diary	Beaulencourt	20/11/1917	20/11/1917
War Diary	Le Bucquiere	21/11/1917	23/11/1917
War Diary	Havrincourt	24/11/1917	30/11/1917
Miscellaneous	Special Divisional Order	28/11/1917	28/11/1917
Miscellaneous	D.A.G. Base Herewith War Diary for the month of December 1917		
War Diary	Havrincourt	01/12/1917	03/12/1917
War Diary	Boyelles	04/12/1917	09/12/1917
War Diary	St-Leger	10/12/1917	29/12/1917
War Diary	Mory	30/12/1917	31/12/1917
Miscellaneous	H Q 119th Infty Bde	16/12/1917	16/12/1917
War Diary	Mory	01/01/1918	31/01/1918
Miscellaneous	D.A.G., 3rd Echelon		
War Diary	Mory	01/02/1918	22/02/1918
War Diary	Nr 4. Camp N. Hendecourt	23/02/1918	27/02/1918
War Diary	Bellacourt	28/02/1918	28/02/1918
Heading	12th Battalion Yorkshire Regiment (Tee-side Pioneers) March 1918		
War Diary	Bellacourt	01/03/1918	11/03/1918
War Diary	Nr 4 Camp Hendecourt	12/03/1918	20/03/1918
War Diary	Hendecourt	21/03/1918	21/03/1918
War Diary	Hamlin Court	22/03/1918	22/03/1918
War Diary	Gomiecourt	23/03/1918	25/03/1918
War Diary	Douchy-Les-Ayette	26/03/1918	26/03/1918
War Diary	Bienvillers-Au-Bois	27/03/1918	27/03/1918
War Diary	Beaudricourt	28/03/1918	29/03/1918

War Diary	Tinques	30/03/1918	30/03/1918
War Diary	Monchy Breton	31/03/1918	31/03/1918
Miscellaneous		28/03/1918	28/03/1918
Miscellaneous	Copy 1/7	30/03/1918	30/03/1918
Heading	12th Battalion Yorkshire Regiment. (Tee-side Pioneers) April 1918		
War Diary	La Rue du Bois	01/04/1918	02/04/1918
War Diary	Bac St Maur	03/04/1918	11/04/1918
War Diary	Strazeele	12/04/1918	13/04/1918
War Diary	Staple Area	14/04/1918	14/04/1918
War Diary	Salperwick	15/04/1918	21/04/1918
War Diary	West Becourt	22/04/1918	30/04/1918
Miscellaneous	XV Corps	19/04/1918	19/04/1918
Miscellaneous	Narrative of operations from 12.0 midnight 8/9th April to 12-0 midnight 11/12th April 1918.		
Miscellaneous	40th Div. No 1115/22 (b) O.C. 12th Yorkshire Regt (Q)	23/02/1918	23/02/1918
Miscellaneous	D.A.G. 3rd Echelon		
War Diary	Kinder Belck	01/05/1918	09/05/1918
War Diary	Esquelbecq	10/05/1918	15/05/1918
War Diary	Les Cinqrues	16/05/1918	31/05/1918
Miscellaneous	D.A.G. 3rd Echelon		
War Diary	Les Cinqrues Near Bollezeele	01/06/1918	22/06/1918
War Diary	La Belle Hotesse	23/06/1918	28/06/1918
Miscellaneous	12th Battalion Yorkshire Regiment (P). Nominal Roll of Officers Postes Appx VII		
Miscellaneous	12th Battalion Yorkshire Regiment (P). Nominal Roll of W.O.s. N.b.O.s and Men		

WO 951260 13

40TH DIVISION

12TH BN YORKSHIRE REGT
(PIONEERS)
JUN 1916 - JUN 1918

ABSORBED BY 17 WORCS BN

12th YORKSHIRE REGIMENT (TEESIDE PIONEERS)

I.E. Satinder

From
O.C.
12th York Regt (Pioneers)

To
Officer i/c
A.G. Office
Base

Herewith War Diary of this Battalion for Month of June.

1/7/16

Lieut Colonel
Commdg 12th (S) Bn Yorks Regiment
(Tees-side Pioneers)

Army Form C. 2118

P/40
Vol 1

WAR DIARY
or
INTELLIGENCE SUMMARY

(Erase heading not required.)

12th (SERVICE) BATT. YORKS REGT.

12TH (S.) BN.
YORKSHIRE REGT.
(TEES-SIDE PIONEERS)
JUL 1 1916
No. ....

Instructions regarding War Diaries and Intelligence Summaries are contained in F.S. Regs, Part II. and the Staff Manual respectively. Title Pages will be prepared in manuscript.

Place	Date	Hour	Summary of Events and Information	Remarks and references to Appendices
PIRBRIGHT	27.5.16		Battalion mobilized.	
SOUTHAMPTON	1.6.16	b.15 p.m.	Embarked on S.S. "INVICTOR"	
HAVRE	2.6.16	9.0 a.m.	Landed HAVRE and proceeded to No 1 rest Camp.	
"	3.6.16	6.3 p.m.	W, X, Y Coys and Transport entrained at Pt 1. "Z" Coy 2 hours later at Pt 6.	
LILLERS	4.6.16	12 NOON	1st train arrived. Detrained and marched to RELY. "Z" Coy 6 hours later.	
RELY	4.6.16	2.20 p.m.	Arrived RELY and billeted in Village. "Z" Coy arrived at 7.45 p.m.	
do	5.6.16		Billeted in village.	
do	6.6.16		do	
do	7.6.16		do	
do	8.6.16		do	
do	9.6.16	14.0 o'c	"Z" Coy left for attachment to 1st Div.	
FOUQUIERES	10.6.16		W & Y H.Q's left and marched to FOUQUIERES and Billeted in village. attached to 15th Div.	
"	11.6.16		W & Y H.Q's Billeted in village. "X" Coy left RELY for attachment to 16th Div. at MAZINGARBE.	
"	12.6.16		Billeted in village. W Coy working on Village line near CHAPEL HILL from 8 - 14. Y Coy from 14 - 20.	
"	13.6.16		do do	
MAZINGARBE	14.6.16	20 o'c	moved to MAZINGARBE. W & Y Coys by motor lorries. Y Coy marched from work in VILLAGE LINE. Billeted in Huts. H.Q's. W & Y Coys now attached to 16th Div for instruction, but continued work on village line for this day only.	
do	15.6.16		Night work for all Coys. W Coy on VILLAGE LINE under orders from 31st ARMY TROOPS COY. X Coy working with R.E on Front line trenches digging communication shelters? Y Coy carrying party carrying equipment trench? up to X Coy.	
do	16.6.16		W & X, Y Coy carrying parties. Carrying Equipment stores up to front line	
do	17.6.16		W & Y Carrying parties. X Coy digging trench and completing excavation. 1 Sgt wounded. (Y Coy)	
do	18.6.16		50 men from W & X Coy carrying parties. remainder men resting	

WAR DIARY or INTELLIGENCE SUMMARY

Army Form C. 2118
12th (SERVICE) BATT. YORKS. REGT. YORKSHIRE REGT.
JUL 1 1916
(TEES-SIDE PIONEERS)

Commdg 12th (S) Bn Yorks Regiment (Tees-side Pioneers)
Lieut Colonel

Place	Date	Hour	Summary of Events and Information	Remarks
MAZINGARBE	19.6.16		Carrying parties of 70 men from W & Y Coys. Remainder of W & Y Coys working on VILLAGE LINE.	
do	20.6.16		Y Cy resting. W Cy working on new C.T. from LONDON ROAD to new fire trench. X Cy left MAZINGARBE for attachment to 11th HANTS (P) at LOOS.	
do	21.6.16		Y Cy resting. W Cy completed C.T. trench.	
do	22.6.16		Half Y Cy making Tm E emplacements other half making W Cy night work on LONDON ROAD VILLAGE LINE. Shortening parapets, making firesteps, enduring zig-zags, five branch and clearing field of fire.	
do	23.6.16		W Cy night work Repairing POSEN ALLEY. Deepening BROADWAY C.T. in fire trench. ½ Y Cy day work making & repairing dug outs in SEAFORTH ALLEY, BLACK WATCH ALLEY and reserve trenches near LOOS.	
do	24.6.16		½ Y Cy continuous work on POSEN ALLEY. ½ platoon Y continuous work on dug outs. Remainder night work deepening C.T. SCOTTS ALLEY and making overhead cover in HARRISON'S CRATER.	
do	25.6.16		Y Cy making dug outs in front & outpost lines LOOS and in by day. 80 men by night deepening communication trenches in VILLAGE LINE. W Cy working on reserve trenches near LOOS. X Cy working on reserve trenches. (1 man wounded)	
do	26.6.16		Ponies from huts into shelters in the tram. W Cy night work deepening C.T. near KENS ROAD. Y Cy night work on NORTHERN up RAILWAY ALLEY. Deepening trenches. Absorbing Tm E emplacement, 9 dug outs on junction VILLE AGE LINE - RAILWAY ALLEY. X Cy LOOS working on reserve trenches. (1 man wounded)	
do	27.6.16		W Cy deepening PRESITE PASSAGE and having duck boards towards LONDON ROAD. Y Cy continued work, digging dug outs making T&M trenches village fire system M.	
do	28.6.16		Y Cy deepening trench S of LENS RD. Digging T heads in VILLAGE LINE & of LENS R.O.W.Cy. PRESIT G' PASSAGE and LONDON RD. Deepening C.T. trench and laying Duck Boards. X Cy work in front of R trenches.	
do	29.6.16		All Coys resting. X grass Bm from LOOS. (1 man killed, 1 wounded loading trucks), 5 am shelled at M2ingarbe 2 men slightly wounded.
do	30.6.16		The Bm concentrated at Houchin Camp.	

2.E. 10 a g
3rd Echelon

Herewith War Diary for
Month of July 1916.

1/8/16 [signature] Lieut. Colonel
Commdg 12th (S) Bn Yorks Regiment
(Tees-side Pioneers)

48 July
Army Form C. 2118
Vol 2

WAR DIARY
or
INTELLIGENCE SUMMARY

12th (SERVICE) BATT. YORKS. REGT.

(Erase heading not required.)

Place	Date	Hour	Summary of Events and Information	Remarks and references to Appendices
HOUCHIN	1.7.16		In rest Camp. H.R.	
do	2.7.16		do	
SOUTH MAROC	3.7.16	12.15am	Took over billets and work of 8th Welsh R.(P) H.R	
do	4.7.16		Coy Commanders shown over work. W Coy attached one French mineurs Coy. X,Y,Z. working on defences	
			at CALONNE. H.R.	
do	5.7.16		W Coy repairing trenches, X Coy cleaning & revetting CHAPTAL ALLEY & BOYAU CHAPTAL. Y Coy making	
			Commenced work, repairing trench + firebays from HOUDEMONT SWITCH to MEANDER ST. H.R	
			T heads off BROCHE walk making loopholes in CALONNE school. Z Coy Apron wiring in HYDE PARK trench, and	
do	6.7.16		work carried on. X Coy small party on DOUBLE CRASSIER repairing trench. H.R.	
do	7.7.16		W Coy cleaning rump files in PICCADILLY UNION ST. SOUTH ST. TREIZE ALLEY. X Coy repairing TEMPLE ST. completed No 2	
			dummy Stm/ ponds on eve of Y Coy making barricade in CALONNE digging trench and making V- school.	
			Z Coy carrying on work began on 5.7.16. Pioneers tunnel from No 2 Barricade to AMPTHILL TUNNEL. H.R.	
do	8.7.16		work carried on W Coy began repairing fire bays in QUARRY ROAD X Coy's party continuing work on DOUBLE CRASSIER. H.R.	
do	9.7.16		W Coy cleaning trenches. Reforming TREIZE ALLEY. X Coy started on following lines of CALONNE trench deepened	
			Y Coy No 2 Barricade in progress, and new trench in school. Z Coy making trench boards digging	
			into bank of Y Coy trench, tunnel from No 2 Barricade in progress. H.R.	
do	10.7.16		W Coy QUARRY ROAD revetted on both X Coy carried on work stated. Y work in progress.70 apron screen	
			HYDE PARK trench revetted other work in progress. H.R.	
do	11.7.16		All work in progress. X Coy started excavation in fortified house. H.R	
do	12.7.16		W Coy trench boards laid in CALONNE sub. work in QUARRY ROAD continued. X Coy day by day by Boyau Q. tunnel	
			from barricades in progress. Y Coy overhead cover started in school, work on T heads nearly complete. Z Coy also	
			work in progress. H.R.	
do	13.7.16		Work in QUARRY RD. progress. trenches & JERMYN ST on 2 circuit wired fire bays. & Coy work in progress Y Coy	
			work in progress. CALONNE trench to school. Z Coy tunnel from No 2 Barricade completed work delayed by Rom powder	

WAR DIARY or INTELLIGENCE SUMMARY

Army Form C. 2118

12th (SERVICE) BATT. YORKS. REGT.

Place	Date	Hour	Summary of Events and Information	Remarks and references to Appendices
SOUTH MAROC	14.7.16		W Coy. JERMYN ST dugouts, making entrance in QUARRY Road. Barn partly cleared in CALONNE NORD & SUD. X Coy. all work carried on. Y Coy. commenced repairing trench and dugouts round RUE BERTHELOT. Z Coy work in progress. Hougomont switch cleared of debris. K.R.	
do.	15.7.16		W Coy. all work carried on. Y.Z. work at CALONNE in progress. K.R.	
do.	16.9.16		W Coy. No work possible on JERMYN ST owing to shelling. Other work carried on. X Coy. started making sapheads post near BOYAU TEMPLE ST. Other work in progress. Y Coy & Z. all work in progress. K.R.	
do.	17.7.16		Work on QUARRY ROAD & JERMYN ST. carried on. X. work in progress. Y Coy No 2 Barricade finished. Z Coy all work in progress. K.R.	
do.	18.7.16		W Coy. Revetting and making dugouts JERMYN ST & QUARRY RD. Work in progress. X Coy finished overhead cover in school in progress. Z Coy. HOUGOMONT SWITCH completed. Other work in progress. K.R.	
do.	19.7.16		Work on QUARRY RD nearly finished. Other work in progress. X Coy "funk" roof put up on demolished house after work in progress. Z Coy began making T. heads from houses to RUE ARAGO and C.T. thence Junction near RUE ARAGO and C.T. SAA chr. HOUGOMONT switch completed. K.R.	
do.	20.7.16		X Coy. cleaned JERMYN ST at debris after shelling. CALONNE NORD & SUD repaired to BAJOLLE line. X Coy. dustbays in shifting have completed. Channel completed No 1 sunken in chicory building finished. Y Coy. revetting CHAPITRE ALLEY. Z Coy. parapets turnpike BUTTERFLY work finished. All other work – progress. K.R.	
do.	21.7.16		W Coy. all work in progress. X Coy work – progress. Y Coy work in school finished. Work on CHAPITRE ALLEY – progress Z. All work in progress. K.R.	
do.	22.7.16		W Coy. started cleaning up NORTH ST. Other work in progress. X Coy all work in progress. Y Coy. work on T. heads between No 1 & 2 Barricades finished. 2 platoons gunroom of NEUF KEEP and EDOUARD KEEP at work to help 14 R.& 9 Highlanders who have 1 Coy away. Z Coy all work – progress. K.R.	
do.	28.7.16		W Coy. started work on TREIZE ALLEY. Other work in progress. X Coy revetment and overhead cover on C.T. finished. One platoon started repairing RESERVE LINE. Y Coy. 2 platoons gunroom of NEUF and EDOUARD KEEPS. Work near CHAPTAL ALLEY – progress. Z Coy. All work in progress. K.R.	

WAR DIARY
or
INTELLIGENCE SUMMARY
(Erase heading not required.)

Army Form C. 2118

12th (SERVICE) BATT. YORKS. REGT.

Place	Date	Hour	Summary of Events and Information	Remarks and references to Appendices
S. MAROC.	24.7.16.		W Coy. All work on CALONNE NORD finished other work in progress. X Coy. All work – fire step. Y Coy. All work in progress. Z Coy. Houjemont trench finished and two houses at N end completed. K.R.	
do	25.7.16.		W Coy. Started deepening PICCADILLY men loos. X. All Indian – TEMPLE ST. finished. Y. work – progress. Z. Started repairing Reserve line working from HAY MARKET towards MAROC. K.R.	
do	26.7.16.		W Coy. All work – progress. X Coy. Y Coy & Z Coy. All work – progress. K.R.	
do	27.7.16.		W Coy. All work in progress. X Coy. Trilithia trench finished. Started work on MAROC defences 2" drive. Y & Z Coy. All work – progress. K.R.	
do	28.7.16.		W Coy. JERMYN ST. finished. X. Y. Z. All work – progress. Two platoons – NEUF and EDGEWARE trenches retrench by R.9.S. Litbourdes at bpw. K.R.	
do	29.7.16.		All work in progress. X Coy. started repairing MIDDLE ALLEY. Party of 1 Sh. 25 Men under Capt. Harris took over S. CRASSIER from 13. York R. and carried thru – defences of N. CRASSIER. K.R.	
do	30.7.16.		All work – progress. Y Coy started new trench from DEVINTION ST. to COAL RT. Infantry working party of 150 men helping them on CHAPEL ALLEY & WMMMI near SAPPER ST. K.R.	
do	31.7.16.		All work in progress. Z Coy started repairing CARFAX RD. K.R.	

From O.C 12th York Regt
To DAG
3rd Echelon

Herewith War Diary for Month of August 1916.

1/9/16   [signature]
                Lieut Colonel
Commdg 12th (S) Bn York Regiment
      (Teesside Pioneers)

Army Form C. 2118

VOL 3

WAR DIARY
or
INTELLIGENCE SUMMARY
(Erase heading not required.)

12th (SERVICE) BATT. YORKS. REGT

Instructions regarding War Diaries and Intelligence Summaries are contained in F.S. Regs., Part II. and the Staff Manual respectively. Title Pages will be prepared in manuscript.

Place	Date	Hour	Summary of Events and Information	Remarks and references to Appendices
SOUTH MAROC	1.8.16		All work in CALONNE, 1st and MAROC Defences and repairing of main communication trenches in progress.	
do	2.8.16		Capt Harris bombers on Double CRASSIER relieved by similar party under 2/Lt Cooper. All work in progress. MIDDLE ALLEY shelled, work hindered.	
do	3.8.16		All work in progress. New trench from Deviation St to Coal St dug. Working party of infantry still helping. Y Coy - CALONNE.	
do	4.8.16		All work in progress.	
do	5.8.16		Capt Harris & party of bombers relieved 2/Lt Cooper on Double CRASSIER. Z Coy shelled refouring D61 main SOUTH STREET. Other work in progress.	
do	6.8.16		All work in progress. Sgt Tindale wounded on DOUBLE CRASSIER	
do	7.9.16		X Coy started repairs on BUTTERFLY WALK, TEMPLE ST and HOUGHMONT ST. W Coy finished drawing TREZE ALLEY started in HOGEWARS ROAD. All work in progress.	
do	8.8.16		X Coy completed Lewis gun emplacement near Chimey Corner. Z Coy SOUTH ST. cleared from entrance to HAYMARKET. One platoon reconstructing dug outs at LES BRÉBIS for Divisional bomb store. Other work in progress.	
do	9.8.16		All work in progress. Z Coy started refouring fire bays off SOUTH ST1	
do	10.8.16		Bombers under Capt. HARRIS on DOUBLE CRASSIER relieved at 5 am by 11th K.O.R.L. All work in progress.	
do	11.8.16		All work in progress	
do	12.8.16		All work in progress	
do	13.8.16		do	
do	14.8.16		CARFAX ROAD trench in Reserved. All work in progress.	
do	15.8.16		All work in progress. X Coy completed all work near Chimney Corner. Started dug out in HORSE GUARDS AVENUE. Men LENS Rly for Signal Coy. working 3 hr shifts.	

WAR DIARY
or
INTELLIGENCE SUMMARY

Army Form C. 2118

12th (SERVICE) BATT. YORKS. REGT

Place	Date	Hour	Summary of Events and Information	Remarks and references to Appendices
S MAROC	16.8.16		All work in progress. X Coy started T.M. emplacement for 2" gun in CHARTAR ALLEY. CARFAX ROAD finished. W Coy started refacing SEVENTH AVENUE.	
do	17.8.16		All work in progress.	
do	18.8.16		X Coy started T.M. emplacement for 2" gun in HORTON RD	
do	19.8.16		Z Coys work on O.G.1, RESERVE line and in CHLORINE held up. Dorm T.M. emplacements for 2" guns begun by Z Coy. No C.4 in L'POOL ST. No C.1. up Bayou 19. No C.2. off Bayou 16. No R4 off Bayou 10. No R3 in front line near Bay 82. No R2 in support line near junct with NEOF ALLEY. No A1 in EDGEWARE ROAD near junct with support line. Y Coy finished refacing COAL ALLEY. LINTHORPE RD opened. Y Coy started refacing BIRDCAGE WALK from BOX TUNNEL to junct with TAMWORTH TRENCH	
do	20.8.16		All work in progress 15 R.R.M.C. men attached to W Cy for work.	
do	21.8.16		Work on T.M. emplacements hampered by lack of M.M.M. frames.	
do	22.8.16		Work on C.4 T.M. Emplacement delayed through hostile fire. CARFAX ROAD thinned in and refaced.	
do	23.8.16		Reliefs for reaction relieved 119th R Bde No 8 Cy in T.M. emplacements. C1. C2 C3. & C4. in CHLORINE Reqdwires. Work on C.4. T.M. emplacement in abeyance. Other work in progress. Infantry working parties in CHLORINE stopped.	
do	24.8.16		C4 T.M. emplacement attacked as owing to hostile fire other work in progress.	
do	25.8.16		All work in progress.	
do	26.8.16		All work in progress.	
do	27.8.16		OUTPOST TRENCH mended with bt'n props. Work continued on 13' 6' bn MAROC Reqdwires. Bm frost tent continued on LESSE'S CROSSING. All work in progress.	
do	28.8.16			
do	29.8.16		All work in progress.	
do	30.8.16		H.Q.'s (less H.Q. Section) X and Y Crys relieved H.Q.'s and 2 Coys 17. N.F. (P) as part of garrison of LOOS. Col Bowes took over duties as Commandant LOOS at 2 p.m. All works CHLORINE RedWires handed over to	
do	31.8.16			

M.Welsh. Lieut Colonel
Commdg 12th (S) Bn York's Regiment
(Tees-side Pioneers)

DAG.
3rd Echelon

Herewith War Diary for
Month of Sept. 1916.

1/10/16.   [signature]
                            Lieut Colonel
          Commdg 12th (S) Bn Yorks Regiment
                (Tees-side Pioneers)

WAR DIARY or INTELLIGENCE SUMMARY

Army Form C. 2118

12th (SERVICE) BATT. YORKS. REGT.

VOL 4

Place	Date	Hour	Summary of Events and Information	Remarks and references to Appendices
LOOS	1.9.16		Nothing to report	
do	2.9.16		L.G. Section and W Coy relieved by Section 17th N.F. and one Coy 13th Corps Cyclists as part of Garrison of Loos. Coys were situated as follows W Coy C. & D. keeps. X Coy A B & E keeps. Y Coy B East and West keeps. Z Coy in S MAROC. H.Q.rs in C keep. Only #/25 of men allowed outside keeps at a time (the following) C.T.'s one under repair. HAY HILL. BOYAU Bq. BUNS ST. CAMERON ALLEY and HAY MARKET. All very bad. Z Coy continues work on T.M. emplacements and bomb store les BREBIS. Major TORTON appointed Town Major of MAROC.	
do	3.9.16		Bomb store at les BREBIS stopped. Men put on to T.M. emplacements. 100 men W Coy sent back to MAROC. 100 cyclists remainder in keeps C & D. Enemy ???? new of SEAFORTH CRATER at 8 p.m. stood to.	
do	4.9.16		Z Coy started new fire trench from H.Q of BLACK WATCH ALLEY through SEAFORTH ALLEY to head of GORDON ALLEY. Repair of HAY HILL stopped.	
do	5.9.16		100 men W Coy relieved 100 men Cyclists in C and D keeps.	
do	6.9.16		100 men W Coy started work on early trench near enclosure.	
do	7.9.16		All work in progress.	
do	8.9.16		- do -	
do	9.9.16		- do -	
do	10.9.16		- do -	
do	11.9.16		- do -	
do	12.9.16		- do - 2/Lt. Col. Walker transferred to England (sick).	
do	13.9.16		Z Coy commenced 2" T.M. emplacement in SEAFORTH ALLEY. W Coy finished work on CABLE TRENCHES.	
do	14.9.16		Clearing up of STREET. HAYMARKET DUKE ST. commenced. Draft of 10 O.R. arrived from 87.3 B.D. under Sgt Kendall.	
do	15.9.16		All work in progress.	
do	16.9.16		- do -	

Lieut. Colonel
Commdg 12th (S) B—

WAR DIARY or INTELLIGENCE SUMMARY

Army Form C. 2118

12th (SERVICE) BATT. YORKS. REGT.

(Erase heading not required.)

Place	Date	Hour	Summary of Events and Information	Remarks and references to Appendices
LOOS	17.9.16		All work in progress. Repairs to Scots Alley commenced.	
-do-	18.9.16		All work in progress.	
do	20.9.16		Party of 3 O.R. received from 37.I.B.D. All work - progress.	
do	21.9.16		All work - progress.	
do	22.9.16		— do —	
do	23.9.16		B Coy stood relieved to PIONEER TRENCH (the new trench dug by them by BLACK WATCH ALLEY to GORDON ALLEY).	
do	24.9.16		All work in progress. B Coy making new shaft & solent tunnel for ventilation and sleeping accommodation	
do	25.9.16		Draft of 3 O.R. received from 37.I.B.D.	
do	26.9.16		All work in progress.	
do	27.9.16		— do —	
do	28.9.16		— do —	
do	29.9.16		— do — Since the Bn came to LOOS. All main C.T. trenches have been repaired and sumps have been dug up to support line. Shafts improved - away men have a bunk. Work in keeps confined to repairs. Still a lot of work to do in B. Keep East and West. Repairs to main roads in LOOS in progress.	
do	30.9.16		All work in progress.	

M. White
Lieut Colonel
Commdg 12th (S) Bn York's Regiment
(Tees-side Pioneers)

Y.P.
C/19
D.A.G.
3rd Echelon

Herewith War Diary for month of
Oct 31
~~September~~ 1916.

[signature]

1/11/16

Lieut Colonel
Commdg 12th (S) Regiment

Army Form C. 2118

WAR DIARY
or
INTELLIGENCE SUMMARY

(Erase heading not required.)

12th (SERVICE) BATT. YORKS. REGT.

Vol 5

Instructions regarding War Diaries and Intelligence Summaries are contained in F. S. Regs., Part II. and the Staff Manual respectively. Title Pages will be prepared in manuscript.

Place	Date	Hour	Summary of Events and Information	Remarks and references to Appendices
Loos	1.10.16		All work in progress.	
do.	2.10.16		do. delayed by wet weather.	
do	3.10.16		— do —	
do	4.10.16		Lt R.A. CRAIG. M.O. i/c. wounded. All work in progress. Lt G. K. DAVIS R.A.M.C. reported for duty. Capt. POMEROY transferred to ENGLAND (sick).	
do	5.10.16		All work in progress.	
do	6.10.16		do.	
do	7.10.16		2 new T.M. emplacements started in CHALK PIT WOOD. All work in progress. PIONEER trench badly blown in by hostile T.M. - is being repaired.	
do	8.10.16		All work in progress.	
do	9.10.16		Reliefs as per Appendix A took place.	See Appendix A
do	10.10.16		Repairs to RAILWAY ALLEY and CHALK PIT ALLEY in progress.	
do	11.10.16		All work in progress.	
do	12.10.16		— do —	
do	13.10.16		II Coy moved from MAROC into billets in PHILOSOPHE. They are responsible for all C.T. from VILLAGE LINE to SUPPORT LINE in HOLLUCH Sector. Lt CRAIG. R.A.M.C. M.O. i/c. Bn. returned to duty.	
do	14.10.16		Repairs to MIDDLE ALLEY started. All work in progress.	
do	15.10.16		— do —	
do	16.10.16		All work in progress.	
do	17.10.16			

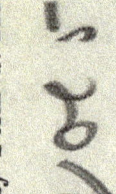

Army Form C. 2118

12th (SERVICE) BATT. YORKS. REGT.

WAR DIARY
or
INTELLIGENCE SUMMARY

(Erase heading not required.)

Instructions regarding War Diaries and Intelligence Summaries are contained in F. S. Regs., Part II. and the Staff Manual respectively. Title Pages will be prepared in manuscript.

Place	Date	Hour	Summary of Events and Information	Remarks and references to Appendices
Loos.	18.10.16.		All work in progress.	
do.	19.10.16.		Very wet. many falls in the trenches. two shelters for infantry started in SEAFORTH ALLEY.	
do.	20.10.16.		Clearing falls in C.T. Shelters finished in SEAFORTH ALLEY.	
do.	21.10.16.		All work in progress	
do.	22.10.16		- do -	
do.	23.10.16		- do -	
do.	24.10.16		Wet day. many falls in trenches.	
do.	25.10.16.		All work - progress.	
do.	26.10.16		- do -	
do.	27.10.16		- do -	
do & MAZINGARBE	28.10.16.	12 noon	Bn. Bn. was relieved by 12th & 3rd SHERWOOD FORESTERS (Pioneers 24th Div.) and proceeded to billets in MAZINGARBE.	
MAZINGARBE	29.10.16.		Billeted in village.	
do & BRUAY.	30.10.16	10 a.m.	Marched to BRUAY and billeted in village.	
BRUAY & MARQUAY	31.10.16	9.30 a.m	Left BRUAY and marched to MARQUAY and billeted in village.	

[signature] Lieut. Colonel
Commdg 12th (S) Bn Yorks Regiment
(Tees-side Pioneers)

Operation Order No 1
by
Lieut Colonel HW Becher
Comm^{dg} LOOS Defences

Appendix p.

1. The following reliefs will take place on Monday 9/10/16 commencing at 8 a.m.
   (a) Z Coy will relieve Y Coy in B. Keep EAST & WEST.
   (b) Y " " " X " " E and A KEEPS.
   (c) X " " will move to MAROC and take over Z Coy's billets.
   Reliefs will go on simultaneously, a small party (1 Officer 10 O.R.) being left behind in each KEEP to hand over to the incoming company.

2. NORTH ST will be used by Z Coy to LOOS.
   PICCADILLY " " " " "X" " from ".

3. O.C. X, Y & Z Coys must make a preliminary reconnaissance of work etc which they are taking over.
   The T.M. emplacement in SEAFORTH ALLEY must not be stopped.

4. X Coys tools, kit etc will be loaded up on 2 G.S. Wagons & 1 empty ration limber on night 8/9 Oct, and proceed to LES BREBIS on same night, and to MAROC on night 9/10 Oct.

   Z Coys tools kits etc will be loaded up on 2 G.S. Wagons and 1 empty ration limber on night 8/9 Oct, and proceed to LES BREBIS same night and to LOOS on night 9/10 Oct.

   As there are a good number of tools etc on charge of B KEEP any tools which Z Coy do not require at LOOS will be loaded up on 1 G.S. Wagon and left at LES BREBIS.
   Blankets will be carried by the men.
   Z Coy's Field Kitchen will move to LES BREBIS on night 8/9 Oct
   X " " " " " MAROC " 9/10 "

5. Rations for Z & X Coys will go to MAROC & LOOS respectively on night 8/9 Oct, and each man will carry one days rations for 9th Oct.

6. X Coys men on Hd Qrs will be attached to Z Coy for rations.
   3 Men of other units at the SOUP KITCHEN will be attached to Y Coy for rations.

Divisional Observers — 3 men on 15 pdr at MAROC will be attached to X Coy for rations.

Coy Sanitary Men and stretcher bearers will move with their Coys.

Lewis Gunners and Keep Signrs will be rationed by the keeps in which they are employed.

O.C. X & Z Coys will hand over to each other a list of men attached to their respective Coys for rations.

7. Completion of reliefs to be reported to this office.

4.10.16.   K. Ridley

Copies to O.C Coys
        2nd in Command.
        C.S.O.
        Q.M
        S.O
        2 War diary

Y.P.
4/36

Officer i/c
Records

Herewith duplicate War Diary for
month of November 1916.

1/12/16.   [signature]
               Lieut. Colonel
               Commdg 12th (S) B. Y. Regiment

Army Form C. 2118

WAR DIARY
or
INTELLIGENCE SUMMARY
(Erase heading not required.)

12th (SERVICE) BATT YORKS REGT

Vol 6

Place	Date	Hour	Summary of Events and Information	Remarks and references to Appendices
MARQUAY	1.11.16		Billeted in village.	
MARQUAY & MONCHEAUX	2.11.16	9.18 am	Left MARQUAY and marched to MONCHEAUX and billeted in village.	
MONCHEAUX	3.11.16		Billeted in village.	
MONCHEAUX & BONNIERES & BOUVOIR	4.11.16	9.0 am	Left MONCHEAUX and marched to BONNIERES. H.Qrs, W; and always billeted in BONNIERES, Bowspot, Y and Z Coy in BOUVOIR.	
BONNIERES BOUVOIR & OUTRE BOIS	5.11.16	10 am	Left BONNIERES and BOUVOIR and marched to OUTRE BOIS and billeted in village.	
OUTRE BOIS	6.11.16		Billeted in village.	
do	7.11.16		Billeted in village.	
do	8.11.16		– do –	
OUTRE BOIS & MONTIGNY	9.11.16	8.30 am	Left OUTRE BOIS and marched to MONTIGNY and billeted in village.	
MONTIGNY	10.11.16		Billeted in village.	
MONTIGNY & MONTRELET	11.11.16	11. am	Left MONTIGNY and marched to MONTRELET and billeted in town.	
MONTRELET & BEAUVAL	12.11.16	10 am	Left MONTRELET and marched to BEAUVAL and billeted – Town.	
BEAUVAL & DOULLENS	13.11.16	10 am	Bn less Z Coy left BEAUVAL and marched to billets in DOULLENS.	
DOULLENS & BAYENCOURT	14.11.16	10 am	Bn less 2 Coy. left DOULLENS and marched to BAYENCOURT and billeted in village. Took over workshops & work etc. from 1/2nd West Riding Coy R.E. Z Coy marched from BEAUVAL to VAUCHELLES to work under C.E. XIII Corps. The Bn is now attached to 31st Div. but works under orders of 120 Bde who held HEBUTERNE Sector.	
BAYENCOURT	15.11.16		6 platoons commenced work on C.T.'s in HEBUTERNE. Remainder next unit.	

Army Form C. 2118

WAR DIARY
or
INTELLIGENCE SUMMARY

12th (SERVICE) BATT. YORKS. REGT

(Erase heading not required.)

Instructions regarding War Diaries and Intelligence Summaries are contained in F.S. Regs., Part II. and the Staff Manual respectively. Title Pages will be prepared in manuscript.

Place	Date	Hour	Summary of Events and Information	Remarks and references to Appendices
BAYENCOURT.	16.11.16.		W.Y.Z. Coys stoked work on C.T's and CROSS TRENCH in HEBUTERNE Sector. X Coy commenced building huts near VAUCHELLES-LES-AUTHIE under C.E. XIII corps.	
do	17.11.16.		All work in progress.	
do	18.11.16.		- do -	
do	19.11.16.		- do -	
BAYENCOURT & HALLOY.	20.11.16.	9.15 am	Left BAYENCOURT and marched to HALLOY and billeted in huts.	
HALLOY.	21.11.16.		Billeted in huts.	
HALLOY & AUTHIEULE.	22.11.16.	9.15 am	Left HALLOY and marched to AUTHIEULE and billeted in huts.	
AUTHIEULE & BERNEUIL.	23.11.16.	9.45 am	Left AUTHIEULE and marched to BERNEUIL and billeted in village.	
BERNEUIL & AILLY-LE-HAUT-CLOCHER.	24.11.16.	9.30 am	Left BERNEUIL and marched to AILLY-LE-HAUT-CLOCHER and billeted in village.	
AILLY-LE-HAUT-CLOCHER.	25.11.16.		Billeted in village. Resting.	
-do-	26.11.16.		- do -	
-do-	27.11.16.		Platoon training commenced.	
-do-	28.11.16.		Platoon training in progress.	
-do-	29.11.16.		- do -	
do	30.11.16.		- do -	

1875 Wt: W593/826 1,000,000 4/15 J.B.C. & A. A.D.S.S./Forms/C. 2118.

DAG
3rd Echelon

Forewith War Diary for Month
of December 1916.

1/1/17

Lieut Colonel
Commdg 12th (S) E. Yorks Regiment
(Tees-side Pioneers)

WAR DIARY or INTELLIGENCE SUMMARY

Army Form C. 2118

12th (SERVICE) BATT. YORKS REGT (PIONEERS)

Vol 7

Place	Date	Hour	Summary of Events and Information	Remarks and references to Appendices
RILLY-LE-HAUT CLOCHER.	1.12.16		Platoon training in progress.	
- do -	2.12.16		- do -	
- do -	3.12.16		Resting.	
- do -	4.12.16		Platoon training in progress.	
- do -	5.12.16		- do -	
- do -	6.12.16		- do -	
- do -	7.12.16		- do -	
- do -	8.12.16		Transport left 8.30 a.m. and marched to LONGPRÉ and billeted in village.	
- do -	9.12.16	4.15 a.m.	Bn. less transport marched PONT REMY and entrained to MERICOURT. L'ABBÉ marched from MERICOURT to BRAY and billeted in Town. Transport marched from LONGPRÉ and joined Bn. at BRAY	
BRAY.	10.12.16	9.0 a.m.	Left BRAY and marched to MAUREPAS camp and billeted in huts.	
MAUREPAS.	11.12.16		Improving billets etc. attached to 4th Dn. for rations and under orders of C.E. XV Corps for work.	
- do -	12.12.16		Improving billets and dug-outs.	
- do -	13.12.16		W 9 X commenced repairs to COMBLES - FREGICOURT road. 7 Coy commenced repairs to COMBLES. RANCOURT road. Z Coy started repairs to COMBLES - RANCOURT road.	
- do -	14.12.16		All work in progress.	
- do -	15.12.16		- do -	
- do -	16.12.16		- do -	
- do -	17.12.16		- do -	
- do -	18.12.16		- do -	
- do -	19.12.16		- do -	
- do -	20.12.16		- do -	
- do -	21.12.16		- do -	
- do -	22.12.16		- do -	

WAR DIARY or INTELLIGENCE SUMMARY

Army Form C. 2118

12th (SERVICE) BATT. YORKS. REGT. (PIONEERS)

Place	Date	Hour	Summary of Events and Information	Remarks and references to Appendices
MAUREPAS	22.12.16		Work on COMBLES-RANCOURT and COMBLES-FREGICOURT roads - progress.	
-do-	23.12.16		-do-	
-do-	24.12.16		-do-	
New MAUREPAS B.20.a.1.? (about there)	25.12.16	11 am	Relieved 19th Battn MIDDLESEX Regt PIONEERS 33rd Division. Casualties during work on roads. 3 O.R. Rfmd. 9 O.R. wounded. 11th PIONEERS 4th Division took over old billets. Rd. Division and supplied 40th Division. 218th BM WEST YORKSHIRE	
-do-	26.12.16		Work begun. W. Coy night work clearing ABODE TRENCH. X Coy day work clearing AGILE TRENCH. Both trenches knee deep in mud in places. Y Coy making fascines roads & draining existing road near HOSPITAL WOOD. Z. Coy laying on duck board track from LE FOREST to near RANCOURT. All work in progress.	
-do-	27.12.16		2 Platoons Z Coy started work on AGILE trench near flu TUNNEL.	
-do-	28.12.16		-do- Duck board track completed.	
-do-	29.12.16		-do-	
-do-	30.12.16		-do- Whole of Z. Coy working in AGILE trench. Trench waist deep in water & mud in places.	
-do-	31.12.16		-do-	

WAR DIARY or INTELLIGENCE SUMMARY

Army Form C. 2118

12th (SERVICE) BATT. YORKS. REGT. (Teesside Pioneers)

Vol 8

(Erase heading not required.)

Place	Date	Hour	Summary of Events and Information	Remarks and references to Appendices
Nr MAROEUIL	1.1.19		All work in progress. W Cy cleaning ABODE LANE (Rancourt Sector) & new trench is being dug from Bn H.Q. to Coy H.Q. old trench too bad to repair. X and Z Cys cleaning AGILE AVENUE. Y Cy making special road near HOSPITAL WOOD.	
-do-	2.1.19		All work in progress. X Cy sent 30 men to ANDOVER to make dug-outs.	
-do-	3.1.19		-do-	
-do-	4.1.19		-do- 1 Platoon Y Cy commenced building shelters at CRANIERS	
-do-	5.1.19		-do- Lt Col H. W. Becker mentioned in Gen¹ Sir D. Haig's dispatch dated 13th Nov. 1916 (New Year's Honours Gazette).	
-do-	6.1.19		-do- 2/Lt FOWLER evac. to England (sick)	
-do-	7.1.19		-do- Two platoons "Y" Cy commenced dug-out in HOSPITAL VALLEY.	
-do-	8.1.19		-do- X Cy now have 2 off. & 83 men living at ANDOVER.	
-do-	9.1.19		-do-	
-do-	10.1.19		-do- AGILE AVENUE now clear to BETHUNE ROAD.	
-do-	11.1.19		-do-	
-do-	12.1.19		-do- Draft of 40 men arrived 10 p.m. from 37th Inf. Base Depot, ETAPLES	
-do-	13.1.19		-do-	
-do-	14.1.19		-do-	
-do-	15.1.19		-do- Major J.C. Wilkinson assumed command of the Bn vice Lt.Col H.W. Becker acting C.R.E.	
-do-	16.1.19		-do- Capt. E. E. Naylor evacuated to England (sick).	
-do-	17.1.19		-do-	
-do-	18.1.19		-do-	
-do-	19.1.19		-do-	

WAR DIARY or INTELLIGENCE SUMMARY

Army Form C. 2118

12th (SERVICE) BATT. YORKS. REGT. (Teesside Pioneers)

Place	Date	Hour	Summary of Events and Information	Remarks and references to Appendices
Mᶜ MURRAY'S	20.1.19		All work in progress. W Coy cleaning and widening ABODE LANE to left Coy H.Q. (RANCOURT SECTOR). X and Z Coys cleaning, draining and widening AGILE AVENUE (BOUCHAVESNES North Sector). Y Coy. Making dug-outs in HOSPITAL WOOD VALLEY, laying FASCINE road and making cupolas at CRANIERS.	
- do -	21.1.19		All work in progress. AGILE AVENUE now cleaned to RIDERSHOT.	
- do -	22.1.19		- do - . Draft of 35.O.R. arrived 10 p.m. from 39 I.B. Depot. ETAPLES	
- do -	23.1.19		- do -	
- do -	24.1.19		- do -	
- do -	25.1.19		- do -	
- do -	26.1.19		- do -	
Camp 14 & Camp 23	27.1.19		The Bn. was relieved by 22ⁿᵈ D.L.I. (PIONEERS) of Division. H.Q. and W Coy moved to Camp 14 on BRAY-CORBIE road about 3 miles from BRAY. X & Y, Z Coys moved to Camp 23. (dug-outs & huts) on CURLU-MERICOURT road. 1/Lt. Ruskin measured grave of Bᵗⁿ Casualties during past - BOUCHAVESNES NORTH and RANCOURT sector 50.R. KILLED 1.Q.O.R. wounded. (Ominoden C.S.M. WORKESTONE Sgt Col. Killed) Posting.	
- do -	29.1.19		W. Coy commenced pulling down huts in Camp 14 with a view to moving them to a new site on BRAY-CORBIE road about ½ miles N. of BRAY. X, Y, Z Coys repairing dug-outs 3 m. as ordered to Gt. Dv. for rations and C.E. XV Corps for work.	
- do -	30.1.19		do	
- do -	31.1.19		do	

JW Silver
Major
Officiating in Command 12th (S) Bn York's Regiment
(Tees-side Pioneers)

Army Form C. 2118

Instructions regarding War Diaries and Intelligence Summaries are contained in F.S. Regs., Part II. and the Staff Manual respectively. Title Pages will be prepared in manuscript.

WAR DIARY or INTELLIGENCE SUMMARY

(Erase heading not required.)

12th (SERVICE) BATT. YORKS. REGT (Labour Pioneers)

Vol 9

Place	Date	Hour	Summary of Events and Information	Remarks and references to Appendices
Camp 14 & Camp 23.	1.2.19		W Coy moving Camp 14 from site N. BRAY-CORBIE road (about 3 miles from BRAY) to new site on same road about 8 miles from BRAY. Co. Y. Z. Coys improving accommodation in Camp 23.	
Camp 14 & Nissen huts N. CURLU	2.2.19		W Coy work - progress. X. Y. Z Coys moved from Camp 23 to Nissen huts on CURLU-MARICOURT road.	
-do-	3.2.19		H.Q. & Coy transport moved to Nissen huts near CURLU. W Coy work - progress.	
-do-	4.2.19		W Coy work - progress. X Coy commenced 7 new dug-outs N. LE FOREST on Reserve line. Y. Z Coys making dug-outs.	
-do-	5.2.19		-do- Y Coy carried on work on dug-outs. X & Z Coys making -do-	
-do-	6.2.19		-do- Z -do- X Y -do-	
-do-	7.2.19		-do- Y -do- Z Coy making. X Coy commenced clearing site and erecting Nissen huts N. CLERY-MARICOURT road near CURLU.	
-do-	8.2.19		X & Z Coys work - progress. Work on dug-outs began. Shifts 3 day-cuts shifted to Z Coy. X to Y Coy.	
-do-	9.2.19		All work - progress.	
-do-	10.2.19		-do-	
Nissen huts N. CURLU and MAUREPAS RAVINE	11.2.19		H.Q. Q's (line transport) X & W Coys moved to MAUREPAS RAVINE and took over huts and work (Haricourt sector) from Z Coy. 52nd D.L.I. Pioneers. Of Dn transport moved to Nissen huts N. CURLU. Y and Z Coys continued work on dug-outs under C.E. 5th Corps. Z Coy continued work on Nissen huts.	
-do-	12.2.19		Y & Z Coy work - progress. X Coy making -do- W Coy continued clearing R.BODE LANE.	
-do-	13.2.19		All work - progress. X Coy continued work on dug-outs N. Hospital Wood road.	
-do-	14.2.19		-do- Lt H BLOOM killed in R.BODE LANE.	
-do-	15.2.19		-do-	
-do-	16.2.19		-do- Work on dug-outs N. Hospital Wood Road handed over to O.C. Dn R.E. Z Coy commenced work on ANDES LANE. 2 platoons by day. 2 by night. Dugouts and clearing trench.	

WAR DIARY
or
INTELLIGENCE SUMMARY

Army Form C. 2118

12th (SERVICE) BATT. YORKS REGT (Teesside Pioneers)

(Erase heading not required.)

Instructions regarding War Diaries and Intelligence Summaries are contained in F. S. Regs., Part II. and the Staff Manual respectively. Title Pages will be prepared in manuscript.

Place	Date	Hour	Summary of Events and Information	Remarks and references to Appendices
NISSEN HUTS N. CURLU & MAUREPAS RAVINE	18.2.19		Work on ABODE LANE, RUDES LANE and dugouts (under O.C. 3C units) in progress	
-do-	19.2.19		-do- Owing to thaw & hard frost ABODE LANE has fallen in along the whole length	
-do-	20.2.19		-do-	
-do-	21.2.19		-do-	
-do-	22.2.19		Work on ABODE LANE, RUDES LANE - progress. 1 platoon Z Coy on dugouts (under O.C. X Bde) Y Coy & 3 platoons Z Coy repairing LE FOREST - RANCOURT road.	
-do-	23.2.19		All work in progress	
-do-	24.2.19		-do-	
-do-	25.2.19		-do-	
-do-	26.2.19		-do-	
-do-	27.2.19		-do-	
-do-	28.2.19		-do-	

Richards,
Lieut Colonel
Commdg 12th (S) Bn Yorks Regiment
(Teesside Pioneers)

Herewith War Diary for the Month
of March 1917.

signature

1/4/17

Lieut Colonel
Commdg 12th (S) Bn Yorks Regiment
(Tees-side Pioneers)

WAR DIARY
or
INTELLIGENCE SUMMARY

Army Form C. 2118

12th (SERVICE) BATT. YORKS. REGT.
(TEES-SIDE PIONEERS)

Vol / 0

Place	Date	Hour	Summary of Events and Information	Remarks and references to Appendices
NISSEN huts nr CURLU & MARICOURT RAVINE	1.3.17		W & Y Coy working on ABODE and ANDES LANE. Y Coy and three platoons Z Coy refossing LE FOREST - RANCOURT ROAD. 1 platoon Z Coy working on dug-outs under C.C. Xy Corps.	
- do -	2.3.17		All work - progres.	
- do -	3.3.17		- do -	
- do -	4.3.17		W & X Cys resting, Y & Z Coys work - progres.	
- do -	5.3.17		All work - progres	
- do -	6.3.17		W & X Coy work - progres. Y Coy relieved Coy of 18th MIDDLESEX Regt. Pioneers 33rd Div. in QUARRY near ROAD WOOD. Z Coy relieved Coy of 18th MIDDLESEX Rgt. on HOWITZER and HEM WOODS.	
nr HEM-CURLU Road about Mont Favorite	7.3.17		H.Q'rs a W & X Coys relieved H.Q & 2 Coys 18th MIDDLESEX Rgt. in billets in HEM-CURLU road. Y Coy commenced working MADAME SWITCH and MACARONI TRENCH Z Coy cleaning MAUD trench. Casualties during stay in RANCOURT SECTOR: Lt. BLOOM killed. 5 O.R. wounded.	
- do -	8.3.17		Y & Z Coys work - progres. SS Coy refossing main roads thourgh CLERY. W Coy cleaning MARY trench WURZEL trench and MAUD trench.	
- do -	9.3.17		All work - progres. Lt ALCOCK and 2/Lt ABBOTT evacuated to England sick on 27.2.17. 2/Lt ANDERSON took on duties of T.O.	
- do -	10.3.17		- do - . 2/Lt TAYLOR appointed to G officer vice Lt BLOOM.	
- do -	11.3.17		All work - progres. Y Cy finished working MADAME SWITCH	
- do -	12.3.17		- do - . progres. W Cy. 2 platoons MARY AVENUE. 2 platoons MAUD AVENUE. X Cy Coys are now working on following: W Cy. 2 platoons MARY AVENUE. 2 platoons MAUD AVENUE. Y Cy. 2 platoons working though CLERY. Y Cy. 2 platoons working 2 platoons WURZEL TRENCH. 2 platoons MACARONI TRENCH. Z Cy. 2 platoons MAUD AVENUE. 1 platoon DOUBLE INTERMEDIATE LINE. 2 platoons MACARONI TRENCH. 2 Cy. The trenches are all in a very bad state MAUD trench and 1 platoon MACARONI TRENCH owing to recent rains.	
- do -	13.3.17		All work - progres. 2/Lt MACDONALD evacuated to Rijuana (sick) 7.3.17	
- do -	14.3.17		- do -	
- do -	15.3.17		- do -	
- do -	16.3.17		- do -	

Army Form C. 2118

WAR DIARY
or
INTELLIGENCE SUMMARY
(Erase heading not required.)

12th (SERVICE) BATT. YORKS. REGT.
(TEES-SIDE PIONEERS)

Instructions regarding War Diaries and Intelligence Summaries are contained in F. S. Regs., Part II. and the Staff Manual respectively. Title Pages will be prepared in manuscript.

Place	Date	Hour	Summary of Events and Information	Remarks and references to Appendices
HEM CURLU Road about 1 mile from CURLU	17.3.17		All work in progress.	
-do-	18.3.17		Owing to German retirement all work on trenches and wiring stopped. W & Y Coy repairing CLERY- BOUCHAVESNES road. Z Coy repairing through CLERY. 2 Coy repairing HEM WOOD CLERY road and MONACU CLERY road.	
-do-	19.3.17		-do-	
-do-	20.3.17		Y & W Coy repairing CLERY-ALLAINES road. Other Coys as above.	
-do-	21.3.17		Y Coy repairing CLERY-PERONNE road. W Coy & Z Coy repairing roads through CLERY. 2 Coy repairing MONACU-CLERY road and HEM WOOD - CLERY road.	
BERLIN VALLEY (just East of CLERY)	22.3.17		H.Q. W. X & Z Coys moved to BERLIN VALLEY. Y Coy remained. Road Wood. All Coys employed repairing CLERY-ALLAINES road. 2/LT JENNINGS (Y Coy) & 2/LT CHAMPNEY (Z Coy) arrived from Base.	
-do-	23.3.17		All Coys employed repairing FEUILLAUCOURT-HAUT-ALLAINES ROAD.	
-do-	24.3.17		-do-	
ANDOVER PLACE	25.3.17		The Bn. less transport moved into billets in MARRIERES WOOD and ANDOVER PLACE. Transport remained in CLERY. Coys employed repairing CLERY- FEUILLAUCOURT road.	
-do-	26.3.17		All Coys employed repairing road in MOISLAINS and making diversion road across CANAL Du NORD and joining MOISLAINS- NURLU road hardly across CANAL Du NORD.	
-do-	27.3.17		-do-	
-do-	28.3.17		-do-	
-do-	29.3.17		W Coy employed repairing MOISLAINS-NURLU road. Remainder as above	
-do-	30.3.17		-do-	
-do-	31.3.17		-do- 2/LT TEMPLE.F (W Coy) & 2/LT JOHNSON.H.A. (Y Coy) arrived from base.	

Commdg 12th (S) Bn Yorks Regiment
(Tees-side Pioneers)

Lieut.Colonel.

Herewith War Diary for the month of April, 1917.

1/5/17

[signature]

Lieut Colonel
Commdg 12th (S) Bn Yorks Regiment
(Tees-side Pioneers)

WAR DIARY
or
INTELLIGENCE SUMMARY
(Erase heading not required.)

Army Form C. 2118

12th Service Batt. YORK. REGT
(Pioneers)

12th York Regt.

Place	Date	Hour	Summary of Events and Information	Remarks and references to Appendices
ANDOVER PLACE	1.4.17		W. Coy continued work on MOISLAINS-NURLU ROAD. X,Y,Z Coys continued work on Deviation road from MOISLAINS across canal du nord & joining MOISLAINS-NURLU ROAD near Canal Bridge.	
-do-	2.4.17		W. & X Coys working on MOISLAINS-NURLU ROAD. Y & Z Coys on Deviation road.	
-do-	3.4.17		W. X. & Y Coys working on MOISLAINS-NURLU ROAD. Z. Coy on Deviation road.	
-do-	4.4.17		-do-	
-do-	5.4.17		-do- Deviation Road completed.	
-do-	6.4.17		All Coys working on MOISLAINS - NURLU Road.	
RIVERSIDE WOOD	7.4.17		Bn. moved into tents and bivouacs in RIVERSIDE WOOD.	
-do-	8.4.17		W Coy assisting R.E. to build bridge across canal du NORD near ETRICOURT. X, Y, Z Coys working on ETRICOURT-EQUANCOURT road.	
-do-	9.4.17		-do-	
-do-	10.4.17		-do-	
-do-	11.4.17		2 platoons 'W' Coy helping ## R.E. Remainder of Bn. on ETRICOURT - EQUANCOURT road.	
-do-	12.4.17		-do-	
-do-	13.4.17		All Coys employed on ETRICOURT. EQUANCOURT road.	
-do-	14.4.17		'W' Coy employed on EQUANCOURT- FINS road. Remainder of Bn. on ETRICOURT- EQUANCOURT road.	
-do-	15.4.17		-do-	
-do-	16.4.17		-do-	
-do-	17.4.17		W. Coy, 2 platoons Z Coy & 3 platoons Y Coy on EQUANCOURT. FINS road. X Coy on road joining FINS and FINS - NEUVILLE BOURJONVAL road. 2 platoons 2 & 1 platoon Y Coy on ETRICOURT. EQUANCOURT road.	
-do-	18.4.17		-do-	
-do-	19.4.17		-do-	
-do-	20.4.17		W & X Coy repairing FINS. NEUVILLE BONSORVAL road. Y & Z Coy repairing EQUANCOURT. FINS road.	
-do-	21.4.17		-do-	

WAR DIARY or INTELLIGENCE SUMMARY

Army Form C. 2118.

12th (SERVICE) BATT. YORK. REGT.
(Teesside Pioneers)

Commdg 12th Bn York's Regiment
(Tees-side Pioneers)
Lieut Colonel

Place	Date	Hour	Summary of Events and Information	Remarks and references to Appendices
RIVERSIDE WOOD	22.4.17		W & C Coy. improving FINS. NEUVILLE - BONSURAH Road	
-do-	23.4.17		-do-	
-do-	24.4.17		-do-	
-do-	25.4.17		Coys improving roads as above till 12 noon. Different communication trench from Q.23.b. 1. 2. to old German front line in V.19.b. (about 1500x) (Night work) constructing from N.19.a. central near BEAUCAMP and VILLERS PLOUICH	
-do-	26.4.17		3 Coys digging C.T. as above. Z Coy moved into tents and bivouacs on ground East of FINS (V.III.b)	
-do-	27.4.17		-do- Z. Coy moved into tents and bivouacs in DESSART WOOD. (W.2.a.)	
-do-	28.4.17		Communication trench is a.m. moved down to depth (4'6") 4 platoons widening C.T. by day. W Coy moved to tents & bivouacs on ground East of FINS (V.III.b.) X & Z Coy commenced digging new trench behind old German wire from about Q.18.b.0.2. to Q.16 central (night work) This line will be known as Bn Intermediate Line.	
-do-	29.4.17		H.Q.s & Y Coy moved to tents & bivouacs near FINS. W. & Z. continued digging Bn Intermediate Line. W Coy Left portion of Intermediate Line.	
V.III.b. Nr FINS	29.4.17		Y Coy widening new C.T. by day. X & Z Coy digging Bn Intermediate line from two C.T. and dugs & drain from new C.T.	
-do-	30.4.17		Establishment Strength etc. beginning of month	

Strength at beginning of month
Off 32 O.R. 834
31 814.
1(Coy)
Drafts received during month. Nil
Casualties

Capt A Stowers. to England (sick). Capt Stephenson resumes command of Y Coy.
Lt McGREGOR R.A.M.C. takes over duties of M.O. vice
Capt. CRAIG to England (sick).
Major TURTON and Lt FEATHERSTONE rejoined the Bn. Works Bn having broken up.
Major TURTON appointed 2nd in command of the battalion on Feb 6th 1917.

Act of Courage. The G.O.C. fourth Army wishes to express his appreciation of the courage and devotion to duty displayed by 21365 Pte H RACE 12th York R. in advancing ammunition on the occasion of an enemy attack.

A5834 Wt. W4973/M68; 750,000 8/16 D. D. & L. Ltd. Forms/C2118/13.

(Copy).   H.Q. 40th Division No C/79/A

C.R.E. 40th Division.
H.Q. 119th Infantry Brigade.
H.Q. 120th Infantry Brigade.
H.Q. 121st Infantry Brigade.
O.C. 12th Yorkshire Regiment.
O.C. 40th Divnl. Works Battn.

The following message received from Commander-in-Chief is repeated for the information of all ranks:-

"I heartily congratulate the Royal Engineers of the Fourth Army on the result of their recent efforts in restoring communications under difficult circumstances."

The Corps Commander has expressed to the Major-General his appreciation of the valuable assistance rendered by the Pioneers and Infantry of this Division.

(Signed) A.L. Cowtan
Captain
D.A.A. & Q.M.G.
40th Division.

H.Q. 40th Division.
4th April, 1917.

(Copy of Telegram received.)
21/4/17.

To. UMPIRE.

Sender's Number.   Day of Month.
G.B. 245.   21st.

Following wire just received from Corps aaa Begins aaa Following received from Commander in Chief Congratulations 15 Corps and 8 and 40th Divisions successful operations carried out this morning aaa In forwarding this the Army Commander desires to add his best thanks to both Divisions for their success aaa and from Usher G.

From. USHER. G.

Y.P.
14/21.

D.A.G.
Base.

Herewith War Diary for the month of May, 1917.

[signature]

Lieut Colonel
Commdg 12th (S) Bn Yorks Regiment
(Tees-side Pioneers)

1/6/17.

WAR DIARY
or
INTELLIGENCE SUMMARY

Army Form C. 2118.

3rd Made 69 I.B.
12th (SERVICE) BATT. YORKS. REGT.
(Kensian Pioneers).

Place	Date	Hour	Summary of Events and Information	Remarks and references to Appendices
Nr FINS (V.II.b)	1.5.17		Y Coy widening new C.T. per day. W Coy Z digging on Intermediate Line behind VILLERS PLOUICH	
- do -	2.5.17		- do -	
- do -	3.5.17		W X Y digging Intermediate line. W. & Z Coy digging Intermediate line behind BEAUCAMP	
- do -	4.5.17		- do -	
- do -	5.5.17		Y Coy repairing FINS - NEUVILLE-BOURJONVAL Road	
- do -	6.5.17		- do - W. X. Y. Z. Coy workings	
- do -	7.5.17		W. X. Y. Z Coys digging Intermediate line near 15 RAVINE	
- do -	8.5.17		Y Coy cleaning roads in GOUZEAUCOURT for HEAVY ARTILLERY. W X/Y Coy diggin Intermediate Line	
- do -	9.5.17		Y Coy repairing FINS-NEUVILLE-BOURJONVAL Road. W. & Z Coys digging Intermediate Line	
- do -	10.5.17		- do - W.X.Z Coy digging C.T. to front line from Rd of 15 RAVINE W.&Z Coy digging front line between BEAUCAMP & BILHEM. X & Y Coy diggin front line in front of VILLERS PLOUICH	
- do -	11.5.17		W.X.Y.Z Coys digging front line in front of VILLERS PLOUICH	
- do -	12.5.17		W.X.Y.Z Coys completing C.T. started 7.5.17	
- do -	13.5.17		W.X.Y. Coys digging fire-bays in C.T. & Z coy deepening same up 12.5.17	
- do -	14.5.17		W.X.Z Coys digging fire trench from head of 15 RAVINE to GOUZEAUCOURT Rd. Y coy cleaning & deepening C.T.	
- do -	15.5.17		W.X.Y.Z coys on INTERMEDIATE LINE & SWITCH behind GONNELIEU	
- do -	16.5.17		W.X.Y.Z widening & deepening above	
- do -	17.5.17		W.X.Y coy continued MEUNIER SWITCH X.5.a - X.9.c Z coy deepening C.T. in R.21.c	
- do -	18.5.17		W.X.Y coy continuing MEUNIER SWITCH. Z coy digging new C.T. in R.20.a	
- do -	19.5.17		W.(X.Y) Coys commenced new C.T. from front line to TARGELLE RAVINE (X.16.central) Z coy continuing SWITCH behind GONNELIEU	
- do -	20.5.17		W.X.Y Coys continuing C.T. in TARGELLE RAVINE. Z coy continuing GONNELIEU SWITCH	

WAR DIARY or INTELLIGENCE SUMMARY

Army Form C. 2118

Ref. Map 57°C. S.E.

12th (SERVICE) BATT. YORK. REGT.

(Two-sided Process)

Place	Date	Hour	Summary of Events and Information	Remarks and references to Appendices
Nr FINS(V.11.A)	21.5.17	(NIGHT)	W. X. Y coys continued MEUNIER SWITCH back to VILLERS-GUISLAINS ... HONNECOURT ROAD. Z coy improving & digging fire-bays in GONNELIEU SWITCH.	
"	22.5.17		W. X. Y coys continuing MEUNIER SWITCH. Z coy commenced digging fire-trench between INTERMEDIATE LINE & GONNELIEU.	
"	23.5.17		Y & Z coys continuing. Fire trench behind GONNELIEU started by Z coy. W & X had night off preparing to move.	
"	24.5.17		W & X coy moved up to the SUNKEN ROAD in W.9.a. W & X continued fire trench behind GONNELIEU at night. Y & Z had night off preparing to Y coy moving. W & X had night off to complete their billets. Y & Z continued fire trench behind GONNELIEU.	
"	26.5.19		W. continued trench. R. 20. a. 20. d.(6m) bourne M.C.T. from R. 25.a.o.8 toward IS RAVINE. Y. & Z. Coys continued fire trench behind a GONNELIEU.	
"	27.5.19		W. diggers new C.T. from R.14.C.5.8. towards IS RAVINE. Z Coy digging new C.T. past 3rd H.Q.(R19d) to Intermediate Line. Y. & Z Coy continued fire trench behind GONNELIEU.	
"	28.5.19		W Y & Z Coy Same as 27.5.17. Z Coy digging C.T. in Q. 30. b.	
"	29.5.19		— do —	
"	30.5.19		W Coy diggers C.T. from R.14.C.5.8 to IS RAVINE. Z Coy digging C.T. in Q.30.b. & deepening C.T. dug on 27.5.17 Y & Z Coys diggers C.T. from R.33.a.5.8. towards front line.	
"	31.5.17		W. & X Coy Same as 30.5.17. Y & Z Coy deepening and widen in fire trench behind GONNELIEU. Establishment Strength etc.	

Strength at beginning of month.
	O.R.	
	31	814.
	30	804
		28

Drafts received & during month.
	O.R.	
	4	
	2	

Casualties.
Killed.
Wounded.
Evacuated Sick. 1. 24
Other Causes. 8.

Remarks. 2/Lt S.C. HOLMES to England (sick) 23.5.17
Lt COHEN R.A.M.C. took over duty of M.O. vice Lt McGREGOR 30.5.17
Capt Shaw took over command of 'Y' Coy vice Capt Stephenson 17.5.17
The following was mentioned in F.M. Sir D. HAIG's despatch dated 9.4.17 Lt Col H.W. BECHER, Lt W.N. CROSBY, 9468 R.S.M. MILLNER.

W. Whites
Lieut Colonel
Comm'g 12th (S.) Bn Yorks Regiment

> 12TH (S.) BN.
> YORKSHIRE REGT.
> JUL 1 1917
> (TEES-SIDE PIONEERS)
> No. YP N/12

D.A.G.
Base.

Herewith War Diary for the month of June, 1917.

[signature]
Lieut. Colonel
Commdg 12th (S) Bn Yorks Regiment
(Tees-side Pioneers)

Army Form C. 2118

Ref. map. 57C S.E.

12th (SERVICE) BATT. YORKS. REGT.
(TEES-SIDE PIONEERS)

WAR DIARY or INTELLIGENCE SUMMARY
(Erase heading not required.)

Place	Date	Hour	Summary of Events and Information	Remarks and references to Appendices
Nr FINS (V.14.b)	1.6.17	(night)	W Coy digging C.T. from R.14.C.5.9. to 15 RAVINE. X Coy improving C.T. in Q.30.b. Y Coy digging C.T. in right of GONNELIEU. Z Coy digging drains from RESERVE LINE behind GONNELIEU.	
- do -	2.6.17		Same as 1.6.17	
- do -	3.6.17		W Coy deepening & widening C.T. from R.14.C.5.9. to 15 RAVINE. X Coy improving C.T. in Q.30.b. Y & Z Coy deepening & widening C.T. on right of GONNELIEU.	
- do -	4.6.17		W. Y. Z Coy. Same as 3.6.17. X Coy digging new trench in front of 15 RAVINE EAST.	
- do -	5.6.17		Same as 4.6.17	
- do -	6.6.17		— do —	
- do -	7.6.17		Y Coy deepening and widening C.T. on left of GONNELIEU. X Y Z. Same as 4.6.17	
- do -	8.6.17		— Same as 7.6.17. —	
- do -	9.6.17		W Coy deepening INTERMEDIATE LINE also 15 RAVINE. Y Coy continuing trench on right of GONNELIEU. X & Z Coys same as 7.6.17.	
- do -	10.6.17		Y Coy deepening & widening & laying trench boards in C.T. on left of GONNELIEU. W.X.Z Same as 9.6.17.	
- do -	11.6.17		W Coy digging C.T. near 15 RAVINE. X.Y.Z. Same as 10.6.17.	
- do -	12.6.17		Z Coy digging C.T. to B.Y. H.Q near 15 RAVINE. W.Y.Z. Same as 11.6.17.	
- do -	13.6.17		W Coy digging new C.T. to foot line in front of VILLERS PLOUICH (R.7.d.). X Coy deepening C.T. to B.Y. H.Q near 15. RAVINE. Also day parties in C.T.'s on left & right of GONNELIEU. Y deepening & widening trench boards in C.T. on left of GONNELIEU. Z Coy ditto in C.T. on right of GONNELIEU.	
- do -	14.6.17		— do —	
- do -	15.6.17		W X Y Coy Same as 13.6.17. Z Coy digging cable trench behind VILLERS PLOUICH (R.19.d)	
- do -	16.6.17		Same as 15.6.17.	
- do -	17.6.17		Same as 15.6.17.	

Army Form C. 2118

Instructions regarding War Diaries and Intelligence Summaries are contained in F.S. Regs., Part II. and the Staff Manual respectively. Title Pages will be prepared in manuscript.

WAR DIARY
or
INTELLIGENCE SUMMARY

(Erase heading not required.)

12th (SERVICE) BATT. YORKS. REGT.
(TEESSIDE PIONEERS).

Place	Date	Hour	Summary of Events and Information	Remarks and references to Appendices
Nr. FINS.(V.M.b.)	18.6.17	Night	W Coy digging new C.T. in R.R.a. X Coy deepening jn trench in front of RAVINE. also day parties C.T.'s on Right and Left of GONNELIEU. Y Coy digging RESERVE LINE on Right of GONNELIEU. Z Coy digging Cable trench near IS RAVINE	
-do-	19.6.17	"	W Coy notified. X. Day work 2 platoons deepening GONNELIEU SWITCH. 2 platoons day parties in C.T.'s on Right and Left GONNELIEU. Y. + Z. Coy same as 18.6.17.	
-do-	20.6.17	"	W. Coy digging new C.T. in R.R.a. X.Y.Z. Coys same as 19.6.17	
-do-	21.6.17	"	do	
-do-	22.6.17	"	do	
-do-	23.6.17	"	do	
-do-	24.6.17	"	do — Y. Coy Resting.	
-do-	25.6.17	"	Same as 23.6.17.	
W.3.c.5.9.	26.6.17	"	H.Q. and Transport moved to W.3.C.5.9. into huts and shelters. Work same as 23.6.17 for W. X. Z. Coys. Y Coy deepening GREEN (GONNELIEU) SWITCH.	
-do-	27.6.17	"	W. X. Z. Coys same as 23.6.17. Y Coy deepening GREEN SWITCH.	
-do-	28.6.17	"	W Y Z Coys working. X Coy same as 23.6.17. C.T. on Right + Left of GONNELIEU (GRESHAM and GIN AVENUES) and new trench learned to front line.	
-do-	29.6.17	"	W Coy digging C.T. to SURREY RAVINE (R.R.a.) X Coy day work deepening, widening + laying track boards in GREEN SWITCH. 'Housemaid' parties on GIN + GRESHAM AVENUES. Y Coy deepening + widening GREEN SWITCH. (Night work) Z Coy digging and filling in cable trench. W. Y. Z. Coys same as 29.6.17	
-do-	30.6.17	"	X Coy Resting except housemaid parties. W. Y. Z. Coys same as 29.6.17	

Army Form C. 2118

WAR DIARY
or
INTELLIGENCE SUMMARY

12th (SERVICE) BATT. YORKS. REGT.
(TEES-SIDE PIONEERS)

(Erase heading not required.)

Instructions regarding War Diaries and Intelligence Summaries are contained in F. S. Regs., Part II. and the Staff Manual respectively. Title Pages will be prepared in manuscript.

Place	Date	Hour	Summary of Events and Information	Remarks and references to Appendices
	June 1917		Strength.	
			Strength at beginning of month. Off. 30 O.R. 804.	
			" " End " " 30 803.	
			Drafts received during month. — 18.	
			Casualties. Killed — 1	
			Wounded — 13	
			Evacuated Sick — 4	
			At Courses —	
				List of officers and O.R. of 12th Bn YORKSHIRE Regt. who have received honours or mention in the Kings Birthday Honours Gazette 1917.
				Lt. Col. H.W. BECHER. — D.S.O.
				T/Capt. A.C. MILDRED — mention
				T/Lieut. W.N. CROSBY — mention
				9468 R.S.M. W. MILLNER — mention
				19936 Sgt. T. McGANN — D.C.M.
			Lt. COHEN R.A.M.C. transfers to 32nd Div.	
			No M.O. appointed in his place.	
			Sick seen by M.O. from 136th F.A.	

[signature]
Lieut Colonel
Commdg 12th (S) Bn Yorks Regiment
(Tees-side Pioneers)

> 12TH (S.) BN.
> YORKSHIRE REGT.
> AUG 1 1917
> (TEES-SIDE PIONEERS)
> No. YP 16/55

A.A.G.
Base

Herewith War Diary for the month of July, 1917.

[signature]
Lieut Colonel
Commdg 12th (S) Bn Yorks Regiment
(Tees-side Pioneers)

Army Form C. 2118

12th (SERVICE) BATT. YORKS. REGT.
(TEES-SIDE PIONEERS)

WAR DIARY or INTELLIGENCE SUMMARY

Ref map. 57.C. S.E.

Vol 14

(Erase heading not required.)

Place	Date	Hour	Summary of Events and Information	Remarks and references to Appendices
W.3.C.5.9.	1.7.17.		W. Coy deepening, widening & laying trench boards in C.T. to SURREY RAVINE. X Coy homeward portion. GIN and GRESHAM AVENUES, laying trench boards in GREEN SWITCH. Y Coy deepening GREEN SWITCH. Z Coy filling in cable trench in Q.24.d.	
-do-	2.7.17		W.X.Y. Same as 1.7.17. Z Coy deepening & widening fire trench in front of 15 RAVINE WEST (DUN RAVEN TRENCH).	
-do-	3.7.17		W Coy commenced widening and improving C.T. in R.7.a. Z Coy (1 platoon) towards FOSTER AVENUE. Y & Z Coys same as 2.7.17. to commenced improving and laying trench Same as 3.7.17.	
-do-	4.7.17		-do- . Y Coy finished deepening GREEN SWITCH	
-do-	5.7.17		-do- . Y Coy commenced deepening FOSTER AVENUE.	
-do-	6.7.17		-do-	
-do-	7.7.17		-do-	
-do-	8.7.17		-do- . 1 platoon X Coy laying trench boards - RESERVE LINE.	
-do-	9.7.17		W Coy finished C.T. in R.7.a (TAFF VALE AVENUE) and commenced deepening & widening FUSILIER TRENCH. Y Coy filling in cable trench. X Coy day work laying trench boards in FOSTER AVENUE, GREEN SWITCH and RESERVE LINE. Homeward portion - GIN & GRESHAM AVENUES. Z Coy moved from DESSART WOOD to sunken Rd in W.10.b near VAUCELETTE FARM.	
-do-	10.7.17		W & X Coy same as 9.7.17. Y Coy finished filling in cable trench and continued deepening FOSTER AVENUE. Z Coy cleared falls in BROADHURST AVENUE & FRONT LINE near 22 RAVINE also dug front line for 70% and commenced trench from GARDNER BANK to TURNER'S QUARRY.	
-do-	11.7.17		-do-	
-do-	12.7.17		W Coy resting. X. Y. Z. Same as 10.7.17.	

Army Form C. 2118.

12th (SERVICE) BATT. CHES. REGT.
(TEES-SIDE PIONEERS)

WAR DIARY
or
INTELLIGENCE SUMMARY.
(Erase heading not required.)

Instructions regarding War Diaries and Intelligence Summaries are contained in F.S. Regs., Part II. and the Staff Manual respectively. Title pages will be prepared in manuscript.

Place	Date	Hour	Summary of Events and Information	Remarks and references to Appendices
W3.a.5.9.	14.7.17.		W. Coy. burying POPE AVENUE. X Coy day work laying trench boards in RESERVE LINE, GREEN SWITCH, FOSTER AVENUE. 'Havermard' follows in POPE, GIN & GRESHAM AVENUES. Y Coy deepening FOSTER AVENUE & DUNRIDGE TRENCH. Z Coy deepening front line near TURNERS QUARRY.	
do.	15.7.17.		- do - Y Coy finished deepening FOSTER AVENUE.	
do.	16.7.17.		- do - Y Coy making new dublits near VAUCELLETTE FARM. W. Coy. deepening DON RAVEN TRENCH. X Coy same as 15.7.17. Y Coy moved to dublits near VAUCELLETTE FARM. Z Coy commenced deepening continuation of 22 AVENUE. Support was turned head LEITH WALK.	
do.	17.7.17.		W. & X Same as 16.7.17. Y Coy commenced ^	
do.	18.7.17.		Same as 17.7.17.	
do.	19.7.17.		W. & X Coy deepening RESERVE LINE in sight of VILLERS PLOUICH. Y & Z Coy same as 17.7.17.	
do.	20.7.17.		- do -	
do.	21.7.17.		Same as 20.7.17 except 1 platoon X Coy laying trench boards in RESERVE LINE nr. GONNELIEU.	
do.	22.7.17.		Same as 21.7.17.	
do.	23.7.17.		Same as 21.7.17. Z Coy work shelled off. 6 in. work by Hun munenwerfer (2 casualties)	
do.	24.7.17.		Same as 21.7.17. Y Coy completed new SUPPORT LINE to FAMOUS AVENUE. (Foot Root required)	
do.	25.7.17.		W. & Y Same as 21.7.17. Z Coy B platoons working in 22 AVENUE.	
do.	26.7.17.		W. X & Y Coys Same as 21.7.17. Y & Z Coys (two platoons) clearing FAMOUS AVENUE and FRONT LINE near FAMOUS AVENUE after raid by enemy. 1 platoon Z Coy digging trench in front of CHESHIRE QUARRY.	

WAR DIARY
or
INTELLIGENCE SUMMARY

12th (SERVICE) BATT. YORKS. REGT
(TEES-SIDE PIONEERS)

Army Form C. 2118

Instructions regarding War Diaries and Intelligence Summaries are contained in F.S. Regs., Part II. and the Staff Manual respectively. Title Pages will be prepared in manuscript.

(Erase heading not required.)

Place	Date	Hour	Summary of Events and Information	Remarks and references to Appendices
W.3.C.5.9.	28.7.17		W Coy finished off RESERVE LINE on right of VILLERS CHURCH. X Coy. 1 Platoon by day laying trench boards on RESERVE LINE behind GONNELIEU. 3 platoons deepening RESERVE LINE on right of GRESHAM AVENUE. Y Coy. 2 Platoons Revetting SUPPORT LINE between FAWCUS and STERAR AVENUES. Z Coy. 2 Platoons deepening SUPPORT LINE between FAWCUS AVENUE and FRONT LINE near FAWCUS AVENUE.	
-do-	29.7.17		W Coy deepening Reserve line on right of GRESHAM AVENUE. X Coy same as 28.7.17. Y Coy 2 Platoons today deepening SUPPORT LINE. 2 platoon by day revetting front line near FAWCUS AVENUE. Z Coy finished extension of 22 AVENUE and found in front of CHESTER QRY.	
-do-	29.7.17		W & X Coy Same as 28.7.17. 2 Platoons Y revetting.	2 platoons Y Coy & Z Coy meeting jammy in SUPPORT LINE 2 Coy
-do-	30.7.17		W & X Coy Same as 28.7.17. 2 Platoons Y Coy revetting FRONT LINE. Remainder digging new SUPPORT LINE near CIRCUS SWITCH.	
-do-	31.7.17		W & X Coy Same as 30.7.17. Y Coy deepening SUPPORT	Red

Strength
Strength at beginning of month. Off. 30 O.R. 803
           " " end " Mont 39. 777.

Drafts received during Month 3. 21

Casualties. Killed . .
            Wounded . 8 .
            Evacuated Sick 1. 19.
            All Causes 14

M. Archer
Lieut.Colonel
Commdg 12th (S) Bn Yorks Regiment
(Tees-side Pioneers)

2/Lt C. MacDon
2/Lt G.E. LORD
2/Lt G.M. CLARK.

Lt FEATHERSTONE (to hospital)

Capt C.E. TAYLOR Struck off Establishment
of Bn 28.5.17

```
                                    12TH (S.) BN.
                                    YORKSHIRE REGT.
                                    SEP 1 1917
                                    (TEES-SIDE PIONEERS)
                                    No. YP 18/4
```

D.A.G.,
3rd Echelon.

Herewith War Diary for the month of August, 1917.

(signature)

Lieut Colonel
Commdg 12th (S) Bn Yorks Regiment
(Tees-side Pioneers)

WAR DIARY or INTELLIGENCE SUMMARY

Army Form C. 2118

Ref. Map 57c S.E.

12th (SERVICE) BATT. YORKS. REGT.
(TEES-SIDE PIONEERS)

Vol 15

Place	Date	Hour	Summary of Events and Information	Remarks and references to Appendices
W.B.C.5.9.	1.8.17		W. Coy. improving RESERVE LINE N° 32 RAVINE. X Coy 2 platoons by day laying French boards on FOSTER AV. and RESERVE LINE. 2 platoons improving FARM RAVINE French. Y & Z Coys digging SUPPORT LINE from CIRCUS SWITCH. Housemaid parties on PODE, GIN & GRESHAM AVENUES, & GREEN SWITCH.	
-do-	2.8.17		-do-	
-do-	3.8.17		-do-	
-do-	4.8.17		-do-	
-do-	5.8.17		-do - Y Coy small day party on SUPPORT LINE laying boards.	
-do-	6.8.17		-do - W Coy finished RESERVE LINE.	
-do-	7.8.17		W. Coy. commenced digging C.T. from BEAUCAMP SWITCH to SUPPORT LINE. X Y & Z Coy same as 1.8.17	
-do-	8.8.17		-do-	
-do-	9.8.17		-do-	
-do-	10.8.17		-do - one platoon X Coy commenced making billets in GOUZEAUCOURT WOOD. (S)	
-do-	11.8.17		-do-	
-do-	12.8.17		-do - Z Coy digging C.T. from BROADHURST AV. to BICESTER AV.	
-do-	13.8.17		-do-	
-do-	14.8.17		Z Coy mined from VAUCELLETTE FARM to GOUZEAUCOURT WOOD (SOUTH). W Coy digging C.T. from BEAUCAMP SWITCH to SUPPORT LINE. Also small day party laying boards on LINCOLN AV. X Coy laying boards on RESERVE LINE, GREEN SWITCH, FOSTER AV. FARM AV. (by day) also building FARM TR. & SYMES AV. by night. Y Coy digging new SUPPORT LINE from CIRCUS SWITCH to CROW QUARRY. Small day party laying boards on the trench.	
-do-	15.8.17		W X Y Coys same as 14.8.17. Z Coy commenced deepening & improving BEAUCAMP SUPPORT.	
-do-	16.8.17		-do-	

Army Form C. 2118.

WAR DIARY
or
INTELLIGENCE SUMMARY
(Erase heading not required.)

Ref. Map 57 c S.E.

12th (SERVICE) BATT. YORKS REGT.
(TEES-SIDE PIONEERS.)

Instructions regarding War Diaries and Intelligence Summaries are contained in F.S. Regs., Part II. and the Staff Manual respectively. Title Pages will be prepared in manuscript.

Place	Date	Hour	Summary of Events and Information	Remarks and references to Appendices
Le.30.S.9	17.8.17		W Coy began C.T. from BEAUCAMP SWITCH to SUPPORT LINE. Also 1 platoon by day laying boards on the C.T. & on LINCOLN AV. X Coy day parties laying boards and improving trenches. RESERVE LINE, GREEN SWITCH, FOSTER AV, FARM AV, SYMES TR. 1 platoon deepening SYMES TR. by night. Y Coy deepening SUPPORT LINE from CIRCUS SWITCH to CROOK QUARRY. Z Coy deepening and laying boards in BEAUCAMP SUPPORT.	
-do-	18.8.17		-do-	
-do-	19.8.17		-do-	
-do-	20.8.17		-do-	
-do-	21.8.17		-do-	
-do-	22.8.17		W Coy finished digging C.T. from BEAUCAMP SWITCH to SUPPORT LINE. X.Y.Z Coys Same as 17.8.17.	
-do-	23.8.17		2 platoons W Coy deepening VILLAGE SUPPORT. One platoon showing larve in LINCOLN AV. & BEAU CAMP C.T. 1 platoon by day laying boards to BEAUCAMP C.T. Y Coy 2 platoons by day widening and improving SUPPORT LINE from CIRCUS SWITCH to CROOK QUARRY. Also laying boards. 2 platoons deepening CIRCUS SWITCH S. of HIGH ST (by night) Z. & Z Coys Same as 22.8.17. FOSTERS AVENUE completed.	
-do-	24.8.17		Same as 23.8.17.	
-do-	25.8.17		SYMES AV. completed. W & Y.Z Coys Same as 23.8.17.	
-do-	26.8.17		LINCOLN & VENUE completed. One platoon X Coy commenced improving FUSILIER TRENCH. No night parties went out.	
-do-	27.8.17		Day parties as usual. No night parties out. W Coy moved by DECAUVILLE RAILWAY to ROISEL to be attached to 34th Division.	
-do-	28.8.17		W Coy moved to QUARRY in F.29.a (map 36.C) S. PREAM TEMPLEUX la GUERARD. X Coy 2 platoons improving FUSILIER TR. 1 platoon on RESERVE LINE & GREEN SWITCH "deepening". Parties on FARM FOSTER, SYMES, GIN and GREEN AVS. Also RESERVE LINE and GREEN SWITCH. Y & Z Coys same as 23.8.17. Z Coy continued on Coys work laying boards in BEAU CAMP C.T.	
-do-	29.8.17		X.Y.Z Coys Same as 28.8.17.	

WAR DIARY or INTELLIGENCE SUMMARY

Army Form C. 2118.

12th (SERVICE) BATT. YORKS. REGT.
(TEES-SIDE PIONEERS)

Place	Date	Hour	Summary of Events and Information	Remarks and references to Appendices
W.28.C.5.7.	30.8.17		W. Cy. Should to 34 Division. X Cy. 2 platoons on FUSILIER AV. 1 platoon on REGINA LANE and GREEN SWITCH. BIRKENHEAD PUBLIC in FARM. FOSTER SYMES Q.M. and GRESHAM AVENUES. Also BEEKIE LANE and GREEN SWITCH. V Cy. 2 platoons improving CIRCUS SWITCH (½ by day). 1 platoon employed improving PENNING AVENUE. Z Cy. B Coy. Coy. improving BEAUCAMP SUPPORT. 1 platoon by day employed on BEAUCAMP SUPPORT and BEAUCAMP C.T. (rear edge - Y58.a A4).	
ditto	31.8.17		W. & Z Coy. do. 30.8.17. V Cy. & platoons improving BEAUCAMP. 2 platoons (½ by day) employed Beaucamp and improving CIRCUS SWITCH and SUPPORT LINE.	
			Remarks.	
			Strength of Regiment at Work 38 977	
			Officers Other Ranks	
			C.O. 25 782	
			People received during week 4 25 × × Nearly all own men returned	
			2/Lt Fowler A. from hospital or base	
			2/Lt Absher J.H.B.	
			2/Lt Turner R.W.	
			(2/Lt Pollard E.J.)	
			Casualties. O.R.A -	
			Wounded 1 2	
			Sick Evac - 8	
			Lt PR MUSPRATT R.A.M.C. took over duties of	
			M.O. 30.8.17.	

(signature)
Lieut Colonel
Commdg 12th (S) Bn Yorks Regiment
(Tees-side Pioneers)

WAR DIARY or INTELLIGENCE SUMMARY

Army Form C. 2118

Ref map 57.c S.E.
12th (SERVICE) BATT. YORKS. REGT.
(TEES-SIDE PIONEERS)

Vol 16

Place	Date	Hour	Summary of Events and Information	Remarks and references to Appendices
b.B.E.F.	1.9.17		2 Coy 2 platoons improving FUSILIER TR. 1 platoon improving POPE AV. 1 platoon laying boards in RESERVE LINE, GREEN SWITCH. Numerous posts in GIN, GRESHAM, POPE, FARM, FOSTER, SYMES, AVENUES. Also GREEN SWITCH and RESERVE LINE. X Coy 1 platoon (day) widening and improving SUPPORT LINE from CIRCUS SWITCH to CROOK QUARRY. 2 platoons improving DENNING AV. 1 platoon digging continuation of CIRCUS SWITCH S of HIGH ST. Z Coy 1 platoon (day) laying boards to BEAUCAMP SUPPORT. 3 platoons deepening and widening BEAUCAMP SUPPORT. W.Coy absorbed in Bn. HQ. Have used Hunk of position captured on 27.9.17. Also Coy trench behind wire called CLUB TR.	
"	2.9.17		W.Y.Z. Coys same as 1.9.17. X Coy finished laying boards in RESERVE LINE and GREEN SWITCH. Y Coy finished continuation of CIRCUS SWITCH. W.Coy digging C.T. to POND TR. from SUNKEN ROAD now called ONION LANE.	
"	3.9.17		W.Z. Coys same as 2.9.17. X Coy 2 platoons FUSILIER TR. 2 platoons POPE AV. However before same as 1.9.17. Y Coy 2 platoons improving ROBERTS AV. 1 platoon (day) SUPPORT LINE.	
"	4.9.17		W.Coy digging C.T. from R+A post Eastwards X.Y.Z. same as 3.9.17. Z Coy finished deepening and widening BEAUCAMP SUPPORT.	
"	5.9.17		W.Coy 2 platoons digging C.T. from R+A post a platoon going up No 2 post and MARTIN LANE. X Y Coys same as 4.9.17.	
"	6.9.17		Z Coy 2 platoons OXFORD LANE. 1 platoon VILLAGE SUPPORT deepening and widening. W Coy finishing X.Y.Z. same as 5.9.17. Day platoon Z Coy laying boards - OXFORD LANE and VILLAGE SUPPORT.	
"	7.9.17		W.Z. same as 5.9.17. Y Coy 3 platoons DENNING AV. TR. (day) & SUPPORT LINE.	
"	8.9.17		W Coy moved up into CAVALRY BRIDGE and camp - B.Coy RESERVE attached to 22nd N.F. ready to go out and start consolidating immediately objective captured "SHADOW CLEAR". 2 platoons carrying 22" N.F. to dig a FLANK TR. from MARTIN'S POST to POINT just where Right of objective. 2 platoons in story point W of WOOD of the TRENCH AND CAPTURED TRENCH. Casualties 3. X.Y.Z. same as 5.9.17. W.Coy moved into Bn. RESERVE & FERVAQUE TRENCH. Remainder two all day at night day team C.T. from town 6 POST to RAILWAY TR. Casualties 9. (also TEMPLE.E.KULLA 2nd killed in a barn use)	
"	9.9.17		W.Y.Z. same as 5.9.17. After completing work on new C.T. W.Coy moved into Bde RESERVE again. Remainder W.B.P.W. when relieved by III Corps Cyclists Richard's billet and Bn can under orders of C.R.E. 34" DV.	

WAR DIARY or INTELLIGENCE SUMMARY

Army Form C. 2118

12th (SERVICE) BATT. YORKS. REGT (TEES-SIDE PIONEERS)

Instructions regarding War Diaries and Intelligence Summaries are contained in F.S. Regs, Part II. and the Staff Manual respectively. Title Pages will be prepared in manuscript.

(Erase heading not required.)

Place	Date	Hour	Summary of Events and Information	Remarks and references to Appendices
H.B.C.S.T.	10.9.17.		W Coy. 2 platoons improving TUSCULE AY. 2 platoon improving POPE AY Shralmard bertins Same as 19.9.17. Y Coy. 2 platoons DENNING AY. 1 platoon improving ROBERTS and VIEW AVE. Roy portions layon toward DENNING, ROBERTS, POPE and SUPPORT LINE. Z Coy. 1 platoon deepening VILLAGE SUPPORT. 2 platoon's deepening OXFORD LANE. Ray platoon layon under - VILLAGE SUPPORT and OXFORD LANE. W Coy. commenced dugout C.T. - daylight from new H.Q. PEST to FARM TR. by this became 54 man deep 138' of track to an depth of 3ft x 4'ft in 65 minutes.	
	11.9.17.		W.Z.Y.Z. Same as 10.9.17. Z Coy. Completed deepening OXFORD LANE	
	12.9.17		X Y. Same as 10.9.17. Z Coy. 2 Platoon deepening and widening BEAU CAMP SUPPORT beyond OXFORD LANE. Ray Platoon completed laying beacon in OXFORD LANE. Y Coy. completed SUPPORT LINE from ORDON QUARRY to CIRCUS SWITCH. W Coy. demolished old mud C.T. to Front line (VILLERET LANE) by day.	
	13.9.17		W Z. Same as 12.9.17. Y Coy. barely layon wooden - VIEW AY. Rest of Coy. Same as 12.9.17. W. Coy. continued VILLERET LANE by day.	
	14.9.17.		W Y. Z. Same as 12.9.17. Y Coy. demolished widening and deepening DENNING AY. 1 Platoon. 3 platoons by day VILLERET LANE. one by night on Same Front.	
	15.9.17.		Ray jointing platoons Same as 12.9.17. Night platoons working. 269. O.R. from 15th RESERVE BN R.E. transferred to BN & posted to Coys as follows. W.Coy. 85. O.R. Z.Coy. 94.O.R. Y Coy. 99.O.R. Z Coy. 90 O.R.	
	16.9.17.		- do - W. Coy commenced track broaden VILLERET LANE No work	
	17.9.17.		W Z.Y.Z. Same as 12.9.17. Y Coy. improving CIRCUS SWITCH	
	18.9.17		Same as 17.9.17.	
	19.9.17		- do - . W. Coy commenced trak broaden VILLERET LANE	
	20.9.17		- do - . 85 O.R. W.Coy. & 99 O.R. Y Coy. transferred to the YORK R. conducting officer 2nd Lieut MACNAY. 94.O.R. X Coy & 90. O.R. Z Coy transferred to 15 YORK R conducting officer Lieut COOPER.	

Army Form C. 2118.

WAR DIARY
or
INTELLIGENCE SUMMARY.
(Erase heading not required.)

12th (SERVICE) BATT. YORKS. REGT
(TEES-SIDE PIONEERS)

Instructions regarding War Diaries and Intelligence Summaries are contained in F. S. Regs., Part II. and the Staff Manual respectively. Title pages will be prepared in manuscript.

Place	Date	Hour	Summary of Events and Information	Remarks and references to Appendices
M.3.c.5.9.	21.9.17		W/Coy. marched from FUSILIER SUPPORT to (night) relief Bay Batts. Bayso moved into their bivouac support in dugouts & shelters NEW RUSSIAN Road. Same as O/No. 110/1 X/Y Coy. Bivouac. ZIRCUS camp & relief by C/B.B. Coys Bay Batts. Bayso	
	22.9.17		Denning Huts & assault launch. Z Coy. support & support & takeover Support by 6/B. 3 Platoons 3 Platoons by night forming an assault & village supports. W/Coy. on platoon by day taken over and support dugouts.	
	23.9.17		-do-	
			-do- W Coy two platoons commenced work on CLUB LANE (by night)	
	24.9.17	-do-	ROBERTS and DERING Rd. one field 3 platoons on CLUB LANE. I by day two plats. VILLERET LANE	
	25.9.17	-do-	Y Coy. commenced fatigue parties - reliefs by 2 coys. working on supplying SUPPORT LINE B	
			Adj Evening Bombardment Myh body. Y Coy. working.	
	26.9.17		X & Y Coys. Same as 25.9.17. W Coy. 1 platoon 2 coys. commenced improv. success LANE also 3 platoons same as 25.9.17	
			W Coy. relief by Y Coy. Dugouts with shelter trans D.Q. & dug commenced show RUSSIAN RD	
	27.9.17		W & Y Coy. same as 26.9.17. 1 platoon Z coy. commenced relieving LEICESTER No 7 coy forward supporting VILLAGE SUPPORT	
	28.9.17		W & Y Coys. Same as 26.9.17. W Coy. finished VILLERET LANE 1 platoon 2 Coy. commenced deepening and widening PLOUGH SUPPORT.	
	29.9.17		W Coy. relieved B Coy 5th Dn. and relieved in HESSEN huts near H.Q. W & Y Coys as 26.9.17.	
	30.9.17		W Coy. working. Y Coy. finished NEW AV. X & Z Coys Same as 26.9.17	

Army Form C. 2118

WAR DIARY
or
INTELLIGENCE SUMMARY
(Erase heading not required.)

12th (SERVICE) BATT. YORKS. REGT
(TEES SIDE PIONEERS)

Place	Date	Hour	Summary of Events and Information	Remarks and references to Appendices
			Strength — Remarks	
			Strength at beginning of month. Off. O.R.	
			35. 782.	
			End — 33 786	
			Draft of men during month. 402. 369 from 1st (Res) Bn R.E. 33 own men returned	
			Casualties Killed. 1. 3. 2nd Lieut E TEMPLE killed.	
			Wounded. 1. 14. 2 — to a Warr. O.	
			Gas. Sick. — 8.	
			Shr. Concus. — 4.	
			184 O.R. transferred to 1/4 YORK.R.	
			131.	
			Capt H F SHEPPERD 19th R.I.R. (P) joined Bn 19.9.17 and took over duties of 2nd in Command vice Major R.B. TURTON	
			Standfield P.B.	
			Capt G. Thomas. struck of establishment. 2.7.17	
			Lt. A.W. Alcock — " " " 30.7.17	

W.Wilkes. Lieut Colonel
Commdg 12th (S) Bn York's Regiment
(Tees-side Pioneers)

12TH (S.) BN.
YORKSHIRE REGT.
NOV 1 1917
(TEES-SIDE PIONEERS)
No. YP20/25

D.A.G.
  Base.

Herewith War Diary for the month of October, 1917.

H.H. Sheppard, Major
Lieut Colonel
Commdg 12th (S) Bn Yorks Regiment
(Tees-side Pioneers)

WAR DIARY or INTELLIGENCE SUMMARY

Army Form C. 2118

12th (SERVICE) BATT. YORKS. REGT (TEESSIDE PIONEERS)

Place	Date	Hour	Summary of Events and Information	Remarks and references to Appendices
W.3.c.8.9.	1.10.17		W.Coy. 3 platoons by night improving PLOUGH SUPPORT. 1st by day laying boards. X Coy. 3 Platoons by night improving POPE, FUSILIER & NEWPORT TR. 1 platoon by day laying boards in POPE, FUSILIER & NEWPORT TR. Numerous nights in 6th GRESHAM, RILEY, BYNES FOSTER AV., GREEN SWITCH and RESERVE LINE. Y Coy. 1 Platoon by day laying boards in CIRCUS SWITCH, BICESTER AV. WILLIS AV., 2 Platoons by night improving MBE. TR. & MINUS AV. 1 platoon enlarging PIGEON and GORGE path near HQ. Z Coy. 2 Platoons by night improving LEICESTER, 5t QUEENS LANE. 1 Platoon (day laying boards in VILLAGE SUPPORT, QUEENS LANE, LEICESTER AV., QUEENS LANE.	
do.	2.10.17		-do-	
-do-	3.10.17		-do-	
-do-	4.10.17		Day parties out as usual. No night parties out.	
-do-	5.10.17		-do- except Y Coy.	
-de-	6.11.17		Battalion busses run week in tunnels to 11th D.L.I. Pioneers. 20th Div. Y. 97 Coy. moved into HISSEN huts at W.3.c. and handed their huts over to 2 Coys. 11th D.L.I. (P). Remainder of D.L.I. halted in huts at W.3.C.	
-do-	7.10.17		W Coy. moved S. To Coy. & 2 platoons X Coy. improving GOUZEAUCOURT - CAMBRAI road in GOUZEAUCOURT (packing out ruts from sidewalk, pave blocks and filling in with grit.) Z Coy. and 2 platoons X Coy. filling in ?? craters on GOUZEAU COURT - CAMBRAI road N. GOUZEAUCOURT station. This work to under C.E. III Corps.	
-do-	8.10.17		W & Z Coy. same as 7.10.17. Y & 2 platoons X Coy. excavating to shelters at W.S.B. & 2 platoon excavating for Section of R31.C. Working with 224 Coy. R.E.	
-do-	9.10.17		Same as 9.10.17	
-do-	10.10.17		-do- 20th Div. relieved 40th Div. at 10 am. Bn. to attached to 20th Div. for administration and orders from half hour. But working under orders of C.E. III Corps.	
-do-	11.10.17		Same as 8.10.17	

Army Form C. 2118

WAR DIARY
or
INTELLIGENCE SUMMARY

(Erase heading not required.)

12th (SERVICE) BATT. YORK. REGT.
(TEES-SIDE-PIONEERS)

Instructions regarding War Diaries and Intelligence Summaries are contained in F. S. Regs., Part II. and the Staff Manual respectively. Title Pages will be prepared in manuscript.

Place	Date	Hour	Summary of Events and Information	Remarks and references to Appendices
L.3.C.5.7.	12.10.17.		W by 4 platoons of Coy repairing GOUZEAUCOURT-CAMBRAI road. In Gouzeaucourt, picking up road from Villers Plouich and filling in with fresh. 2 Coy & 3 platoons of Coy filling in shell holes on GOUZEAUCOURT-CAMBRAI road near GOUZEAUCOURT station. Y Coy excavating for cupola shelters at W.5.b & R.31.e. 22 of R.E. erecting cupolas. Companies working 6 hours on site.	
-do-	13.10.17		- Same as 12.10.17.	
-do-	14.10.17		- do - Worked 3 hours in the a.m.	
-do-	15.10.17		- do - " 6 "	
-do-	16.10.17		- do - - do -	
-do-	17.10.17		- do - - do -	
-do-	18.10.17	12.30 p.m.	Bn. moved by DECAUVILLE from FINS to PERONNE billeted night in PERONNE. Transport moved by road.	
PERONNE	19.10.17	2 p.m.	Bn. (less transport) entrained at PERONNE FLAMMICOURT station, detrained at SAULTY L'ARBRET and marched to LA COUCHIE and billeted in village. (Officers in houses men in huts). Transport moved by road from PERONNE	
LACOUCHIE			via BAPAUME and billeted there Bn. rejoined 40th Division.	
-do-	20.10.17		Bn. resting. Transport moved from BAPAUME to LACOUCHIE.	
-do-	21.10.17		- do -	
-do-	22.10.17		Parade from 8.30 a.m. to 12.30 p.m. (Plays Avub. platoon drill etc.) afternoon devoted to sports.	
-do-	23.10.17		Bn. resting. (wet day)	
-do-	24.10.17		Same as 22.10.17.	
-do-	25.10.17		- do -	
-do-	26.10.17		- do -	
-do-	27.10.17		- do -	
-do-	28.10.17		Church Parade Service. Transport left LACOUCHIE 10 a.m. & proceeded to BAPAUME & billed there.	
-do-	29.10.17		Transport moved from BAPAUME to MOISLAINS. Bn. (less transport) entrained at GOUY-EN-ARTOIS at 4.45 p.m.	
MOISLAINS	30.10.17		Bn. (less transport) detrained at PERONNE-FLAMMICOORT at 10.a.m. and marched to MOISLAINS and billeted in huts there 3 Coys. in huts HQ & Y Coy in village. Bn. is now administered by III Corps	

1875 Wt. W593/826 1,000,000 4/15 J.B.C. & A. A.D.S.S./Forms/C. 2118.

Army Form C. 2118

WAR DIARY
or
INTELLIGENCE SUMMARY
(Erase heading not required.)

12th (SERVICE) BATT. YORKS. REGT.
(TEES-SIDE PIONEERS)

Instructions regarding War Diaries and Intelligence Summaries are contained in F. S. Regs., Part II. and the Staff Manual respectively. Title Pages will be prepared in manuscript.

Place	Date	Hour	Summary of Events and Information	Remarks and references to Appendices
MOISLAINS	31.10.17		12. X. Y. Coys commenced working Abscon and Tincourt huts C.19.a (ALBERT embroul sheet) Z Coy continued laying of base standings for Rest factory near Peak factory MOISLAINS. This unit is under C. E. III Corps.	
			Strength	
			Strength at beginning of month — off 37	
			" " " " — 33 786	
			" end " " — 38 781.	
			Drafts received during month. 5. 2nd Lt. A.G. ABBOTT rejoined. 2nd Lieuts. T. MCGINLEY, H. BERGHOFF.	
			13. been sent returned. S.F. HUTTON, T.G. WILSON joined from	
			39th I.B.D.	
			Casualties. Killed —	
			Wounded —	
			Evac. Sick — 7 Capt. (a/major) H.E. SHEPPERD,M.C.took over command of "B".	
			Other causes — 10	
			8. 27.10.17. vice Lt. Cl. H.W. BECHER, D.S.O. on leave.	

H.E. Shepperd Major
Lieut Colonel
Commdg 12th (S) Bn Yorks Regiment
(Tees-side Pioneers)

WAR DIARY or **INTELLIGENCE SUMMARY**

Army Form C.2118

12th (SERVICE) BATT. YORKS. REGT. (TEES-SIDE PIONEERS)

Place	Date	Hour	Summary of Events and Information	Remarks and references to Appendices
MOISLAINS	1.11.17		W x Y Coy continued erecting Adrian and Nissen huts. Z Coy continued erecting stables near Sugar Factory MOISLAINS. This work is under O.C. III Corps.	
-do-	2.11.17		No 11 platoon Y Coy (2/Lt Johnson) moved into huts near LONGAVESNES & commenced erecting Adrian & Nissen huts at TEMPLEUX LA FOSSE.	
-do-	3.11.17		-do-	
-do-	4.11.17		2 platoons V Coy moved into Nissen huts at ETRICOURT. Remainder of W.X. Same as 2.11.17.	
-do-	6.11.17		Y Coy moved to LONGAVESNES. 2 platoon W Coy commenced erecting Adrian & Nissen Huts from MANANCOURT.	
-do-	5.11.17		To NURLU. Remainder of work same as 2.11.17. 2 platoons W Coy continued deepening & platoon W Coy and 2 platoons Y Coy erecting huts at MOISLAINS. 2 Platoons W Coy continued deepening pipe track from MANANCOURT to NURLU. 2 platoons Y Coy erecting huts at TEMPLEUX LA FOSSE. Z Coy continued stables at MOISLAINS.	
-do-	7.11.17		W Coy moved to MANANCOURT and commenced erecting huts on MANANCOURT or MANANCOURT - LE MESNIL road. Remainder of work same as 6.11.17.	
-do-	8.11.17		Same as 7.11.17.	
-do-	9.11.17		Remainder of W Coy moved to MANANCOURT. 2 platoon Y Coy moved from MOISLAINS to FINS. 1 platoon Y Coy moved from LONGAVESNES to FINS. X Coy took on W or Y Coy work.	
-do-	10.11.17		Y Coy erecting huts at MOISLAINS. W Coy two platoon erecting huts MANANCOURT one platoon unloading train at ETRICOURT. one platoon on pipe line from MANANCOURT to NURLU. Z Coy continued stables at MOISLAINS. X Coy 1 platoon DECAUVILLE train unloading. Railway materials at FINS, R.E. dumps and proceeding with train and off loading material at MILLERS PLOUGH (Nifty work)	
-do-	11.11.17		Same as 10.11.17. Camp at TEMPLEUX LA FOSSE completed (5 Adrian huts, 6 Nissen huts, Cookhouse, latrine etc.)	
-do-	12.11.17		X Coy and one platoon Z Coy moved from MOISLAINS to camp on MANANCOURT or MANANCOURT - LE MESNIL road. 1 platoon Y Coy moved from TEMPLEUX LA FOSSE to MANANCOURT. Z Coy took over X Coy work. Z Coy completed stables near road (no material available to work). W Coy 2 platoons on pipe line. 2 platoons erecting huts at MANANCOURT. X Coy on platoon Z Coy one platoon Y Coy erecting huts at MANANCOURT. Z Coy erecting huts at MOISLAINS.	
-do-	13.11.17		Same as 12.11.17.	

WAR DIARY **12th (SERVICE) BATT. YORKS. REGT.** (TEESIDE - PIONEERS)

or

INTELLIGENCE SUMMARY

Army Form C.2118

(Erase heading not required.)

Instructions regarding War Diaries and Intelligence Summaries are contained in F.S. Regs, Part II and the Staff Manual respectively. Title Pages will be prepared in manuscript.

Place	Date	Hour	Summary of Events and Information	Remarks and references to Appendices
MORLAINCOURT	14.11.17.		2 platoons W. Cy & X. Cy. 1 platoon Y. Cy 2 Cy. orderly butt to Bde Camps at MANANCOURT. 2 platoon W. Cy on pipe line from MANANCOURT to NURLU. Y Cy loading Railway material on DECAUVILLE & being R.E. dump and proceeding with train and off loading it at VILLERS PLOUICH. 2 Cy. erecting huts at MOISLAINS. Brigade Camps at MANANCOURT and MOISLAINS completed.	
-do-	15.11.17		Y Cy. Fins. One platoon Y Cy moved from MANANCOURT	
-do-	16.11.17.		2. Cy. working W & X Cy on pipe line from MANANCOURT to NURLU Y Cy same as 14.11.17.	
-do-	17.11.17		-do-	
-do-	18.11.17.		-do-	
-do-	19.11.17	4 p.m	Bn left present billets and marched to BEAULENCOURT and billeted in same huts recently used by Div.	
BEAULENCOURT	20.11.17.	10 a.m	Order marked to Bn to be ready to move in one hours notice at 4 p.m. Bn moved to 2 Bn of (LE BOCQUIERE) (maps 57c N.8)	
LE BOCQUIERE	21.11.17		at midnight catn. Bn billeted in clean billets at LE BOCQUIERE at 11. a.m.	
-do-	22.11.17		Q.M & men Bn (two transport & details) proceeded to make road for infantry and pack mules from K.9.0.0.8. along DEMICOURT - GRAINCOURT road to CANAL DO NORD. Bn returned to billets b.p.w. [?]complete (maps 57c N.W.)	
-do-	23.11.17.	4.0 a.m.	Bn moved into billets at HAVRINCOURT assuming at 11. a.m.	
HAVRINCOURT	24.11.17		2 platoons W.Cy & X Cy working on HAVRINCOURT - GRAINCOURT road via K.3.d.7.0. (679 house) 2 platoons W.Cy looking on HAVRINCOURT - GRAINCOURT road direct. Clearing road from mounds filling in miles Road via K.3.d.7.0 made good for traffic to GRAINCOURT. Y Cy 5 platoons making diversion round crater at K.27.d.w.t. (579) location made good for traffic. 1 platoon repairing road from K.27.d.w.t. to square in HAVRINCOURT VILLAGE Z. Cy in Reserve. Casualties W.O.R. wounded.	
-do-	25.11.17.		W & X Cy Same as 24.11.17. Z. Cy repairing diversion round crater at K.27 d.w.t. Y Cy carrying prefabs and wire to DAISY FIELD to R.E. from K.11.b.3.8. to E.23.d.2.9. (579).	
-do-	26.11.17.		W. Cy 2 platoons repairing HAVRIN COURT - GRAIN COURT road via K.3.d.7.0. (579 house). 2 platoons making diversion round previous crater at K.27.c.1.8. X Cy 2 platoons repairing HAVRIN COURT - GRAIN COURT road direct. 2 platoons repairing diversion round crater at K.27.d.w.t. 2 platoon Y Cy carrying wire and prefabs from dumps at K.11.b.3.8. (map 579) S. of GRAINCOURT to front line in BOURLON WOOD. 2 platoon Y Cy to E.29.a.7.8. (map 579) Carrying ma and prefabs from K.11.b.3.8. to E.29.a.7.8. (map 579) Sugar factory on CAMBRAI - BAPAUME Road.	

1875 Wt. W.5193/826 1,000,000 4/15 J.B.C.& A. A.D.S.S./Forms/C.2118.

WAR DIARY or **INTELLIGENCE SUMMARY**
(Erase heading not required.)

Army Form C. 2118

12th (SERVICE) BATT. YORKS. REGT.
(TEES-SIDE PIONEERS)
Ref map 57c. 1/40,000

Comdg 12th Bn Yorks Regiment
(Tees-side Pioneers)

W.H. Hopps
Lieut Colonel

Place	Date	Hour	Summary of Events and Information	Remarks and references to Appendices
HAVRINCOURT	26.11.17	(Coy)	2 platoons Z Coy digging Sec trench with 229 F. Coy R.E. in BOURLON WOOD about F.13.b.4.7. 2 platoons X Coy Whites Coastline Capt J.A. Harris missing.	
"	27.11.17		W & X Coy repairing roads as on 26.11.17. Y Coy digging strong point in BOURLON WOOD with 229 Coy R.E. Z Coy digging Sec trench in BOURLON WOOD about E.7.d.11. Casualties 3 O.R. wounded.	
"	28.11.17		W Coy repairing HAVRINCOURT-GRAINCOURT road in HAVRINCOURT VILLAGE. X Coy repairing HAVRINCOURT-GRAINCOURT road via K.3.a.7.0 and diversion round SNOWDEN CRATER K.27.d.4.1. Y Coy 2 platoons working in BOURLON WOOD with 281 F.G.R.E. & 224 F.Co R.E. about F.7.c.5.5. Z Coy working in BOURLON WOOD from F.13 b.5.9. to F.14.a.0.5. Casualties 2 O.R. killed, 2nd Lieut JOHNSON & 7 O.R. wounded. From 25.11.17 to 28.11.17 (incl) the Bn has been attached to Corps DW for work.	
"	29.11.17		W & X Coy repairing roads same as 28.11.17. Y & Z Coys resting. Battalion is now working under C.R.E. 47th Div. W Coy 2 platoons making redoubt trench from HAVRINCOURT-GRAINCOURT. X Coy repairing HAVRINCOURT -GRAIN COURT road via K.3.d.7.0. Y & Z Coys repairing roads in HAVRINCOURT VILLAGE. All work stopped at 12 noon and Battalion told to "Stand by" owing to GERMAN ATTACK on GONNELIEU and GOUZEAUCOURT.	
"	30.11.17		Strength Remarks.
			Strength at beginning of month. Off. O.R.
			End - 38. 781.
			Drafts received during Month - 43 153.
			Casualties Killed - 7 14
			Wounded - 2
			Gas Side 1. 15* 2nd Lt. W.A. JOHNSON (wounded).* Pte HYDE since died of wounds.
			Other Causes - 30
			- 1. 5 Capt J.A. HARRIS (missing) Lt. J.H. FEATHERSTONE struck off establishment.

2nd Lts TOWETT. S.F. (Z) LARTER. A.S (X) HASEMAN J. (W)
BENTLEY. A.W.B (Y) PROCTOR C.V. (X) DAVISON E. (W)
BOEWING. B. (Z) joined from 37. I.T.B.D.

Copy

Special Divisional Order.

The Commander-in-Chief personally informed the Divisional Commander that he wished all ranks of the 40th Division to be congratulated on his behalf, on their recent success.

Great credit is due, not only to Infantry Brigades who gave proof of fine fighting qualities & endurance, but also to the loyal co-operation & untiring energy shown by the Royal Artillery (including the Div. Ammun. Column,) the Royal Engineers, 12th (S) Batn. Yorkshire Regt. (Pioneers)

Sd. W.G. Charles
Lt Col.
Gen Staff 40th Div.

28. Nov. 1917.

> 12TH (S.) BN.
> YORKSHIRE REGT.
> JAN 31 1917
> (TEES-SIDE PIONEERS)
> No. Y.P. 23/55

D.a.G.
Base

Herewith War Diary for the month of December, 1917.

[signature]

Lieut Colonel
Comdg 12th (S) Bn Yorks Regiment
(Tees-side Pioneers)

WAR DIARY or INTELLIGENCE SUMMARY

Army Form C. 2118

12th (Service) Batt. York & Lanc. Regt. (Teesside Pioneers)

Place	Date	Hour	Summary of Events and Information	Remarks and references to Appendices
HAVRINCOURT	1.12.17		W. X Coys repairing roads from HAVRINCOURT to GRAIN COURT. W Coy making Infantry track from HAVRINCOURT to GRAIN COURT. Y.Z. Coys repairing roads in HAVRINCOURT VILLAGE.	
-do-	2.12.17		-do-	
-do-	3.12.17		-do-	
BOYELLES	4.12.17		Bn. less transport left HAVRINCOURT 8.0 a.m. marched to ROUYAULCOURT entrained there. Detrained at BOYELLES W & Y Coys proceeded to ST LEGER and took over hut's vacated by 11th HANTS R.(P) HQ. X.Z. Coys took over hut's vacated by 11th HANTS R.(P) in BOYELLES CAMP. Transport left HAVRINCOURT 9.30 a.m. & proceeded by march route to BEAUMETZ. Bn. rejoined 40th Division. Bn. nucleus transport rejoined Bn.	
-do-	5.12.17			
-do-	6.12.17		Z. Coy moved to ST LEGER. W.Y.X Coys commenced work on line improving C.T. ————— Y Coy commenced repairs to ST LEGER - CROISILLES - FONTAINE Road. Casualties 1.O.R. Killed 1.O.R. wounded (Y Coy)	
-do-	7.12.17		Z. Coy commenced repairs to C.T. in W. sector. Remainder same as 6.12.17	
-do-	8.12.17		Y Coy moved from BOYELLES to ST LEGER. X.Y.Z. Same as 7.12.17	
-do-	9.12.17		X. Coy less 1 platoon moved from ST LEGER into Caves at CROISILLES. HQ less transport & Q.M. stores moved 15 ST LEGER. 3 platoons Y Coy working in shifts assisting the tunnelling Coy R.E. to make dug-outs in TUNNEL TRENCH. 1 platoon Y Coy continued work on CROISILLES - FONTAINE Road. X.Y.Z. Same as 7.12.17	
ST-LEGER	10.12.17		W Coy X Coy Y Coy continued repairs to C.T. Y Coy same as 9.12.17 1 platoon X Coy moved to CROISILLES	
-do-	11.12.17		Owing to exposed German attacked 3 m block to at 6.30 a.m. X Coy occupied posts in CROISILLES. Remainder stood to in Coy bombs grounded continued work. Same as 11.12.17	
-do-	12.12.17		-do- Owing to enemy barrage many falls in C.T. these were cleared.	
-do-	13.12.17		W. X & Z Coys continued work on C.Ts. fitting A frames etc. 1 platoon of Y Ast. 16 G.S.W. Loads of metal on CROISILLES - ST. LEGER road, lengthening 3 Platoons tunnelling for 174 Tunnelling Coy. R.E. on old GERMAN TUNNEL UNDER TUNNEL TRENCH. W. X. & Z Coy worked as yesterday. 3 platoons of Y with 174 T. Coy. R.E.	
-do-	14.12.17		metal on CROISILLES — ST. LEGER road. At night Capt. C.M. SOUTHEY/ Assist O.C. 229 Coy. R.E. 1 platoon of Y remain platoon hut down 16 Loads to tape out front line trench from U.20.c.5.75 V.20.b.8.3 to be dug on 15.12.17 That HENDECOURT sheet 1:20,000	

WAR DIARY or INTELLIGENCE SUMMARY

Army Form C. 2118

12th (SERVICE) BATT. YORKS. REGT. (PIONEERS)

Place	Date	Hour	Summary of Events and Information	Remarks and references to Appendices
St. LEGER.	15.12.17		1 Platoon of Y. Coy carried wire to JOVE Trib. from V.20.A.87 during day. W. & one platoon of X commenced digging new front line on line after Zero hour (3.30pm) and worked until 8 p.m. Z. & one platoon of X then took over & completed 440 yards of trench with 11 firebays by 2.0 a.m. Remaining 2 Platoons of X coy under Lt. MILLER completed a belt of apron wire in front of Coy 11.0 p.m. No casualties.	
"	16.12.17		W.X. and Z coys continued work on C.T's. One Platoon of Y on CROISILLES - FONTAINE rd and remainder of coy working for 174 T. Coy R.E.	
"	17.12.17		Work to same as yesterday.	
"	18.12.17		" " "	
"	19.12.17		" " " C.T's. Y. Coy deepened & widened 160 yds of new front line. 2 Platoons of X completed formed slopes of apron wire to front of same.	
"	20.12.17		W.X. on C.T's. Y (1 platoon continued road) retaining 3 working for 174 T. Coy R.E. Z coy deepened & widened a further 115 x of new front line. 2 Platoons X completed apron wire in front.	
"	21.12.17		W.X. continued work on C.T's. One platoon of Y on road, remainder on C.T's, boring, revetting, draining etc. Z coy deepening & widening new front line (named PIONEER TRENCH).	
"	22.12.17		Z left each coy drew & filled wire & pickets during day for work at night. Remaining half coys commenced wiring as follows at 4pm :- W. & Y SUPPORT LINE from MARS LANE to PELICAN AVENUE. X & Z FRONT LINE from VULCAN STRONG POINT to TRIDENT ALLEY. Continued work as yesterday.	
"	23.12.17		FRONT LINE wiring completed at night 23 - 24/12/17. SUPPORT needs strengthening.	
"	24.12.17		W & Y (less 1 platoon on CROISILLES - FONTAINE road) completed support line wire. X coy on C.T. 2 improving PIONEER TR.	
"	25.12.17		W.X. & 3 platoons of Y on C.T's, one platoon Y working on road.	
"	26.12.17		Same as 25.12.17.	
"	27.12.17		Work continued on C.T's & road. Considerable enemy shelling. Capt. COOPER & one man slightly wounded.	
"	28.12.17		Work continued on C.T's & road.	
"	29.12.17		H.Q. & Y Coy moved to TUNNELLERS CAMP at MORY, X coy to CAVES in ECOUST. W & Z remained at St LEGER & continued work on C.T's.	
MORY.	30.12.17		Work taken over from 20th K.R.R. Convoy 3rd Division. & proceeded with X coy allowed one platoon off to improve the CAVES.	
"	31.12.17		(signed) .... O.C. Transport & Q.M. Stores rejoined H.Q. from BOYELLES.	

Army Form C. 2118.

WAR DIARY
or
INTELLIGENCE SUMMARY.

12th (SERVICE) BATT. YORKS. REGT.
(TEES-SIDE PIONEERS)

(Erase heading not required.)

Place	Date	Hour	Summary of Events and Information	Remarks and references to Appendices
			Strength	
			Strength of Regiment 6 months: Off 48, OR 158	
			" " " 2nd " : 42, 100	
			Distribution during month — 6 - 9am men returned	
			Casualties	
			Killed — 1	
			Wounded — 3. Capt. Godfrey wounded 21 July, admitted 1 OR 24 July.	
			Sick — 5. 2/Lt. Jackson was to England (not)	
			Gun Course — 1	
			51. 50 or RE men as transferred to R.E. and J. TURNER transferred to R.F.C. on selection	
			Rambles	
			Capt. W.N. CROSBY. 2/Lt. SPENCE. E. STEWARDSON + Sgt. DOUGLAS HAIG'S Hospital	
			Capt STEPHENSON G. transferred to Spec. Bn R.E. 24 G. 28.11.16	

[signature]

Lieut Colonel
Comdg 12th (S) Bn Yorks Regiment.
(Tees-side Pioneers)

H Q
119th Infty Bde.

16.XII.17

Dear Colonel,

Just a line to thank you for the very excellent work yr fellows did for me last night & to congratulate you on having such fine men & officers under yr command.

It was a treat to walk down yr trench after wading (?) down (?) the other!

Yrs sincerely

J H Crozier

WAR DIARY or **INTELLIGENCE SUMMARY**
Army Form C. 2118.

12th (SERVICE) BATT. YORKS. REGT.
(TEES SIDE PIONEERS)

Vol 20

Place	Date	Hour	Summary of Events and Information	Remarks and references to Appendices
MORY	1.1.18.		Work continued in C.T.S. (General repairs) No. 1 platoon X Coy repairing tramway in front of LOCUST & NOREUIL. Left in trenches owing to frost.	
"	2.1.18.		-do-	
"	3.1.18.		-do-	
"	4.1.18.		-do-	
"	5.1.18.		-do-	
"	6.1.18.		-do-	
"	7.1.18.		-do-	
"	8.1.18.		2 platoons X Coy & 2 platoons Y Coy commenced digging new bus track from TANK AV (U.28.b.7.4.) to FOX TROT LANE (U.28.d.6.0.) Remainder of Bn continued general repairs to C.T.S.	
"	9.1.18.		Y Coy & X Coy two plats on tramway maintenance & two on bus track.	
"	10.1.18.		Z Coy moved from ST LEGER to MORY. X Coy two tramway parties, Y Coy, Z Coy continued work on new bus track.	
"	11.1.18.		Work continued on bus track. W Coy took over Z Coy work.	
"	12.1.18.		-do- Commenced continuation of new track from TANK AV to LONDON SUPPORT.	
"	13.1.18. 14.1.18. 15.1.18.		-do-	
"			No work on new track owing to weather. X. & W Coys continued clearing trenches. All C.T. we were taking on and are in a very bad state owing to extremely wet weather.	
"	16.1.18.		No work possible on new TR. W. Coy clearing PELICAN AV & LEG LANE. X Coy clearing BULLECOURT AV. Y. Coy carrying trench boards for track parallel to TANK AV. Z Coy bruning BULLECOURT AV.	
"	17.1.18.		W Coy cleared trench from PELICAN AV & LEG LANE. X Coy cleared TANK AV. Z Coy cleared TANK AV & repairing tramway. Y Coy cleaning SYDNEY AV. Z Coy cleared BULLECOURT AV, & building stables at BURROW CAMP.	
"	19.1.18.		-do-	

WAR DIARY
or
INTELLIGENCE SUMMARY
(Erase heading not required.)

12th (SERVICE) BATT. YORKS. REGT.
(TEES-SIDE PIONEERS)

Army Form C. 2118

Place	Date	Hour	Summary of Events and Information	Remarks and references to Appendices
MORY	20.1.18		W Coy clearing mud from LEG LANE & PELICAN AV. X Coy clearing TANK AV & repairing tramway from SYDNEY AV. Z Coy clearing BULLECOURT AV. & building shelters DURRON CAMP.	
"	21.1.18		- do -	
"	22.1.18		- do -	
"	23.1.18		LEG LANE cleared. W. Coy commenced clearing STAFFORD LANE. X.Y.Z. Coy same as 20.1.18	
"	24.1.18		- do -	
"	25.1.18		- do -	
"	26.1.18		- do -	
"	27.1.18		BULLECOURT AV. & TANK AV. cleared. X.Z. Coy commenced training	
"	28.1.18		SYDNEY AV cleared. Y Coy commenced tramway & then trench W Coy clearing & trimming	
"	29.1.18		STRAY SUPPORT. X YZ Coys same as 29.1.18	
"	29.1.18		- do -	
"	30.1.18		- do -	
"	31.1.18		- do -	

WAR DIARY or **INTELLIGENCE SUMMARY.**
(Erase heading not required.)

Army Form C. 2118.

12th (SERVICE) BATT. YORK REGT
(TEES-SIDE PIONEERS)

Place	Date	Hour	Summary of Events and Information	Remarks and references to Appendices
	JANUARY. 1918.		Strength.	

Off.   O.R.
Strength at beginning of month. 42. 700.
         "   "   end   "   "   31. 573.

Drafts received during month. 1. 119.   97 B.T. men posted from England to replace 100 men transferred to 13th YORK. R.

Casualties. Killed.   -   3.
            Wounded.   -   18.   " " individuals 3 at duty.
            Evac. Sick. 5. 78.   " 31 B.T. men transferred P.B. by A.D.M.S.
            Other Causes. 1.   7.   " 2/Lt McGINLEY transferred to R.F.C.
            Transferred to 13th YORK R. -   100.
            Re-transferred to R.E. -   50.

Remarks. Following officers transferred to England (sick). Capt. CROWE. Lt's DUFF. MILLER. ARMSTRONG.
                                                                                                FOWLER.

Capt. J.H. HARRIS awarded M.C. (New Years honours gazette)
20389 Sgt. & I.I. IRCKSON   -   D.C.M.   -do-
9468 R.S.M. W. MILLNER   -   Belgian CROIX de GUERRE

MMichie.   Lieut Colonel
Commdg 12th (S) Bn.York Regiment
(Tees-Side Pior ETS)

> 12TH (S.) BN
> YORKSHIRE REGT.
> MAR 1 1918
> (TEES-SIDE PIONEERS)
> No. YP 27/75

D.A.G.
3rd Echelon.

Herewith War Diary for the month of February, 1918.

W. Shepherd for Major
Lieut Colonel
Commdg 12th (S) Bn Yorks Regiment
(Tees-side Pioneers)

WAR DIARY or INTELLIGENCE SUMMARY

Army Form C. 2118.

(Erase heading not required.)

Place	Date	Hour	Summary of Events and Information	Remarks and references to Appendices
MORY	1.2.18		W. Coy. general reference to PELICAN Av. & STRAY SUPPORT. X Coy. general reference to TANK Av. and TRAMWAYS. Y Coy. general reference to SYDNEY Av. and ECOUST SUSSEX road. Z Coy. general reference to BULLECOURT Av.	
"	2.2.18		-do.- 100 Coy R.E. withdrawn to R.E. working strength of Coys about 40 O.R.	
"	3.2.18		-do.-	
"	4.2.18		-do.-	
"	5.2.18		-do.- Reference to STRAY SUPPORT & ECOUST-SUSSEX road emptied.	
"	6.2.18		-do.- 1 Platoon Y Coy repairing MORY-ECOUST road. 1 Platoon X Coy commenced tramway deepening NEW TRENCH.	
"	7.2.18		-do.-	
"	8.2.18		-do.- Reference to BULLECOURT Av. completed	
"	9.2.18		-do.- 2 Coys. commenced thinning & deepening NEW TRENCH on right flank Av.	
"	10.2.18		general reference to main communication trenches and continuance on NEW TRENCH on RIGHT FLANK of TANK Av. Reference to MORY-ECOUST road in progress.	
"	11.2.18		-do.-	
"	12.2.18		-do.-	
"	13.2.18		-do.- 4th Bn. relieved in the line by 59th (NORTH MIDLAND) Div. Battn. was attached to 59th Div. for work. Draft of 10 officers 230 O.R. posted to Battn. from 7th (S) Bn. YORKSHIRE REGT. working strength of Coys now about 90 O.R.	
"	14.2.18		general reference to main C.T. continued. NEW TRENCH continued. Reference to MORY-ECOUST road in progress. Work on NEW TRENCH hindered by shell fire casualties 1 O.R. (wounded)	
"	15.2.18		Same as 14.2.18. Reference to SUSSEX VRAUCOURT road and VAULT-MORY road commenced.	
"	16.2.18		Same - -do- 15.2.18	
"	17.2.18		-do-	
"	18.2.18		-do-	

WAR DIARY or INTELLIGENCE SUMMARY

Army Form C. 2118.

(Erase heading not required.)

Place	Date	Hour	Summary of Events and Information	Remarks and references to Appendices
MORY	19.2.18		General repairs to main C.T's Continued. New Fire Trench Continued. Repairs to MORY-ECOUST. SUCRERIE.	
"	20.2.18		-do- MORY COURT and ivory Roads in progress	
"	21.2.18		-do-	
"	22.2.18		-do- Day parties only out working.	
No 4 Camp N HENDECOURT	23.2.18		Batt: relieved by 1/1 ROYAL SCOTS FUSILIERS Pioneers 59th D.N. and moved to No 4 Camp N HENDECOURT by Light Railway. Transport by road. Batt: rejoined half Bn.	
"	24.2.18		Batt: Re-organised into H.Q. & 3 Companies. Z Coy ceased to exist. Officers and O.R. of late Z Coy divided up equally between 10 new Coys.	
"	25.2.18		Coy trainings 9.00 am to 12.30 p.m. Remainder of day devoted to sports	
"	26.2.18		-do-	
"	27.2.18		-do-	
BELLACOURT	28.2.18 2 p.m		Batt. moved by road route to BELLACOURT and billetted in village.	

Army Form C. 2118.

WAR DIARY
or
INTELLIGENCE SUMMARY.

(Erase heading not required.)

Instructions regarding War Diaries and Intelligence Summaries are contained in F. S. Regs., Part II. and the Staff Manual respectively. Title pages will be prepared in manuscript.

Place	Date	Hour	Summary of Events and Information	Remarks and references to Appendices
	FEBRUARY 1918.		Strength.	
				off. O.R.
			Strength at beginning of month. 37. 573.
			" " end " " 45 612.
			Drafts received during " 10. 258. 10 officers 239 O.R. from 7th York. R 19 O.R from Base depot. — 12.2.18
			Casualties
			K.M.d — 1
			Wounded — 3x 3 includes 2 at duty.
			Gas. Sick. 2 59. 2/Lt PROCTOR G.V. + 2/Lt WILKINSON M (to England)
			other Causes — 5
			Re-transferred to R.E. — 100. (1.2.18)
			Remarks. 5 Joining officers transferred from 7th YORK R Capt. WILKINSON.G.D D.S.O. M.C.
			2/ LIEUTS BOTT.S. BYWELL.J. ROYCE.G.H. MERTON.I.H. DEANS.A.V. DOWNS E.L. KING.C.L.
			3 mms 9 WILKINSON M
			Capt G.D WILKINSON D.S.O. M.C. took over command of 'Y' Cy. 13.2.18.

M.W.Haynes (?)
Lieut Colonel
Commdg 12th (S) Bn Yorks Regiment
(Tees-side Pioneers)

40th Divisional Troops.
3/4---

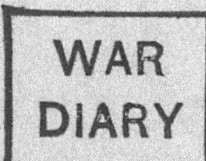

12th BATTALION

YORKSHIRE REGIMENT

(Tee-side Pioneers)

MARCH 1 9 1 8

Army Form C. 2118.

WAR DIARY
or
INTELLIGENCE SUMMARY.

(Erase heading not required.)

12TH (S.) BN. YORKSHIRE REGT. (TEESSIDE PIONEERS)

Instructions regarding War Diaries and Intelligence Summaries are contained in F.S. Regs., Part II. and the Staff Manual respectively. Title pages will be prepared in manuscript.

Place	Date	Hour	Summary of Events and Information	Remarks and references to Appendices
BELL ACOURT	1.3.18		Coy training in morning. Sports in afternoon	
"	2.3.18		- do -	
"	3.3.18		No parade	
"	4.3.18		Coy training in morning	
"	5.3.18		- do -	
"	6.3.18		- do -	
"	7.3.18		Draft of 113 O.R. arrived from Base Depot.	
"	8.3.18		Batt. lion transport inspected by Lt. Gen. Sir AYLMER HALDANE K.C.B. D.S.O. Commanding VI Corps with 121st Bde Group on ground near BAZEUX.	
"	9.3.18		Coy training in morning. Sports in afternoon. Draft of 20 O.R. from 20th Entrenching Battn arrived	
"	10.3.18		Church Parade.	
"	11.3.18		Coy training in morning. Sports in afternoon.	
My Coup HENDECOURT	12.3.18		Bath proceed by march route to new Camp HENDECOURT. Battn under 1/2 hour notice to move from 8 p.m.	
"	13.3.18		No parade. 2 hours public from 9.0 am to 9 pm daily	
"	14.3.18		Coy training in morning. Sports in afternoon. Draft of #2 O.R. arrived from Base Depot	
"	15.3.18		- do -	
"	16.3.18		- do -	
"	17.3.18		Church Parade.	
"	18.3.18		Coy training in morning. Sports in afternoon.	
"	19.3.18		- do -	
"	20.3.18		- do -	

Army Form C. 2118.

12TH (S.) BN.
YORKSHIRE REGT.
1 1918
(TEES-SIDE PIONEERS)
NO........................

WAR DIARY
or
INTELLIGENCE SUMMARY.
(Erase heading not required.)

Place	Date	Hour	Summary of Events and Information	Remarks and references to Appendices
HENRIECOURT	21.3.18		Battalion stood to at 5.30 am owing to German attack 8.30 pm Battalion moved by route march to CHAPPMEL CAMP HAMELIN COURT.	
HAMELIN COURT	22.3.18	10 am	Battalion manned during line in front of village of HAMELIN COURTWITH 224 Field Coy R.E. on left and 229 Field Coy on night. Batt. HQ in CHAPPMEL CAMP. at 3.6 p.m. transport moved to DOUCHY-lès-AYETTE.	
GOMIECOURT	23.3.18	12 noon	Battalion handed over trenches in front of HAMELINCOURT to COLDSTREAM GUARDS 3.0 pm and moved to GOMIECOURT and manned old trenches from ERVILLERS to BEHAGNIES with 224 Field Cy R.E. on right and 9th MANCHESTER R. on left. B.n H.Q. in GOMIE COURT 4.0 pm H W BEEVER D.S.O. wounded.	
		10 p.m	Major H.F. SHEPPERD H.Q. Park was reminder of Battalion hostile shelling active on ERVILLERS, BEHAGNIES LINE, GOMIECOURT heavily shelled from 12:45 pm to 3.0 pm transport moved to BOMMEQUERT.	
		12 m	Battalion entrained (hm) ERVILLERS, BEHAGNIES LINE at 4 pm Enemy withdrawn into RESERVE in GOMIE COURT and utilized to support strong points in rear of ERVILLERS. at 2 p.m transport moved to BELAINZAUVILLE.	
	25.3.18		Battalion continued to hold ERVILLERS, BEHAGNIES LINE. at 5 p.m. H.Q. evacuated GOMIE COURT and moved to COURCELLES le COMTE. At 9.0 p.m enemy attacked trenches held by X and Y Coys. Line retired to follow GOMIE COURT and eventually took up a position in front of COURCELLES where H.Q. moved to DOUCHY-les-AYETTE at 2 am. 26.3.18 at 5 p.m. W.g. found a defensive Park to NORTH of ACHIET-le-GRAND and effected all stragglers by totals eventually 900 men. Lt. C. MACKENZIE wounded. at 4 p.m. MAJOR H.F. SHEPPERD M.C. wounded Major Capt. SOUTHEY took over command of Battalion. at 3 pm transport moved to MONCHT-AU-BOIS.	

A5834 Wt. W4973 M687 750,000 8/16 D. D. & L. Ltd. Forms/C.2118/13.

Army Form C. 2118.

WAR DIARY
or
INTELLIGENCE SUMMARY.
(Erase heading not required.)

YORKSHIRE REGT.
MAR 1918
(TEES-SIDE PIONEERS)

Instructions regarding War Diaries and Intelligence Summaries are contained in F.S. Regs., Part II. and the Staff Manual respectively. Title pages will be prepared in manuscript.

Place	Date	Hour	Summary of Events and Information	Remarks and references to Appendices
DOUCHY-LES-AYETTE	26.3.18		By 2nd MANCHESTER R. Battalion relieved between 2 am and 5 am and marched to DOUCHY-LES-AYETTE and marched to BIENVILLERS-AU-BOIS arriving at 12 noon. Transport arrived at 11 a.m. at 2 p.m. Enemy reported to have broken through at HEBUTERNE. Battn ordered to hold line from WINDMILL in FONQUEVILLERS-BIENVILLERS road to BIENVILLERS-HENNESCAMP road with 121 B.de on RIGHT and 119 B.de on LEFT. at 10.30 p.m. Battalion withdrawn into billets in BIENVILLERS-AU-BOIS. at 2 p.m. Transport moved to POMMIER.	
BIENVILLERS-AU-BOIS	27.3.18	7.30 am	Battalion moved to BEAUDRICOURT and billeted in village	
BEAUDRICOURT	28.3.18		Battalion resting and cleaning up	
"	29.3.18	8.30 am	Battalion moved into billets in TINQUES and TINQUETTE	
"		2.30 pm	Battalion moved into billets in FRONCHY BRETON	
TINQUES FRONCHY BRETON	30.3.18			
	31.3.18	8.15 am	Battalion less transport marched to BERRY and arrived at 2 p.m. at VIEUX BERQUIN and marched to LA RUE DE BOIS DES ROCQUES in Major Beauchant moved to FLEURS.	
La Rue du Bois				

Army Form C. 2118.

WAR DIARY
or
INTELLIGENCE SUMMARY.

(Erase heading not required.)

12TH (S.) BN.
YORKSHIRE REGT.
1918
(TEESSIDE PIONEERS)

Place	Date	Hour	Summary of Events and Information	Remarks and references to Appendices
MARCH	1918		Strength	
			Strength at beginning of month	
			Officers 45 OR 819	
			40 847	
			Services rendered during	
			113 OR from Base Depot 5.3.18	
			20 OR " " " " 9.3.18	
			40 OR " " " " 14.3.18	
			60 OR " " " " 20.3.18	
			19.3.18 6 casuals from Base Depot & hospital (other ranks)	
			Casualties:	
			Killed 3	
			Wounded 3 80 12 OR evacuated & three in hospital at Etaples, wounds	
			Missing 11	
			Sick, 3rd 22	
			At Duty 3 2/Lt Bywater transferred to M.G.C. Capt Porter to Reserve Employed	
			5 64	
			Remarks: Bros O.R. during end of March to reinforcement at Battalion.	

C.Hadley Major
Lieut-Colonel
Commdg 12th (S) Bn Yorks Regiment
(Tees-side Pioneers)

"Copy"

The following extract from a letter written by the Corps Commander to the Divisional Commander is forwarded for your information.

It should be communicated to all ranks.

"As regards your fighting troops, Infantry, Artillery and R.E. I cannot speak too highly. They have made a magnificent defence and, tired as they must be with so prolonged a struggle, they have stood like a stone wall between my right and the Germans.

All I can say is that I am deeply grateful and feel that they have nobly upheld the great fighting traditions of the British Army."

29-31-18   (Sgd). G.H. Chapman
                    for Lt. Col.
                    General Staff, 40th Div.

Issued to all units.

"Copy"

To all Ranks of the 40th Division.

I wish to thank the Division, one and all, for their splendid courage and behaviour.

You know what the Commander-in-Chief and your Corps Commander think of you and I can only say you have done your duty like British Soldiers always do.

We shall no doubt be called upon again to fight for all we are worth.

We in the 40th Division shall be ready again and I feel very proud to be the Divisional Commander of such a splendid body of men as you have proved to be. I thank you all from the bottom of my heart and whatever may happen I feel complete confidence in the ultimate result with soldiers of your spirit and bravery under my Command.

28.3.18   Signed John Ponsonby
                    Major General
                    Commanding 40th Division.

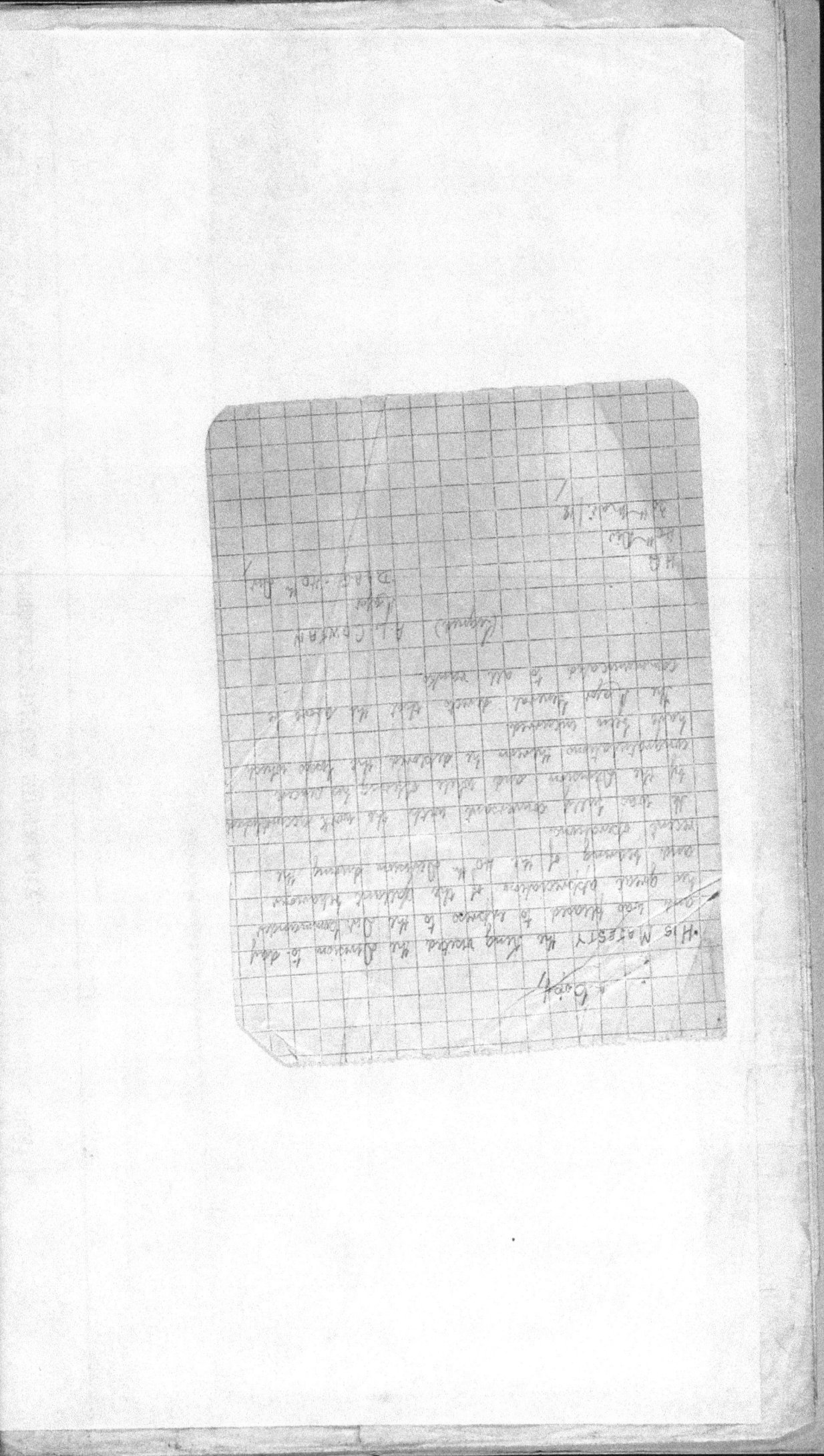

40th Divisional Troops.

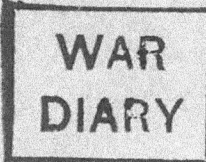

12th BATTALION

YORKSHIRE REGIMENT.

(Tee-side Pioneers)

APRIL 1 9 1 8

Attached :- Report on Operations 8th-12th April

Army Form C. 2118

WAR DIARY
or
INTELLIGENCE SUMMARY.

(Erase heading not required.)

12 Yorkshires

Vol 23

Place	Date	Hour	Summary of Events and Information	Remarks and references to Appendices
LA RUE DU BOIS	3.4.18		Bn. transport arrived from LILLERS & rejoined Battalion.	
	4.4.18	3.30 p.m.	Bn H.Q. and took over Right Sector (by Pioneer 51st Division) H.Q. & "A" & "X" Coy BAC ST MAUR.	
BAC ST MAUR	5.4.18		"W" Coy SAILLY SUR LA LYS. "Y" Coy RUE DE LA LYS. Bn H.Q. HUDOR.	
"	6.4.18		— do —	
"			Work carried on SUBSID. RGY LINE. General reference. 1 platoon X Coy working on tramways in SAILLY area. "Y" & "W" Coy. Working with 145 A.T. Coy. R.E. Nothing to report. Nil Casualties.	
"	7.4.18		— do —	
"	8.4.18		— do —	
"	9.4.18		— do —	
"	10.4.18		— do —	
"	11.4.18		See attached narrative	
STRAZEELE	12.4.18		Concentrated near STRAZEELE came under orders of 119 Inf Bde on arrival	
		10 p.m.	"X" Coy sent out with few posts on the STRAZEELE – CAESTRE & STRAZEELE – FLÊTRE road to limit traffic	
	13.4.18	4 a.m.	"W" & "X" Coys went out to dig a series of Strong Posts on STRAZEELE ridge	
		3 p.m.	Concentrated with 119 Bde near Bn HQ	
		4 p.m.	Moved to LE BREARD from where Bn was ordered to proceed to	
STAPLE AREA	14.4.18	10.30 am	STAPLE Area & billet for the night. Moved by motor lorries to SALPERWICK	
SALPERWICK	15.4.18		Bath, resting & cleaning up Major T H CARLILE DSO MC took over command of Bn.	
"	16.4.18		Companies training in the morning & sports in the afternoon.	
"	17.4.18		— do —	
"	18.4.18		— do —	

WAR DIARY
or
INTELLIGENCE SUMMARY

Army Form C. 2118

Instructions regarding War Diaries and Intelligence Summaries are contained in F. S. Regs., Part II. and the Staff Manual respectively. Title Pages will be prepared in manuscript.

Place	Date	Hour	Summary of Events and Information	Remarks and references to Appendices
SALPERWICK	19.4.15		Companies training in the morning & Sports in the afternoon	
"	20.4.15		do	
"	21.4.15	12 p.m.	Moved by road route to WESTBECOURT. 3 Offrs & 180 O.R. transferred to 5th YORK R. Joined the R's & took over command of "Y" Coy	Majr J. SWEET. & Lg 2 R. W. Fus.
WESTBECOURT	22.4.15		Coys training in the morning. Sports in the afternoon	
"	23.4.15		do. do	
"	24.4.15	12.15pm	Moved out of WESTBECOURT & embus'd at ACQUIN. Orders cancelled en route & returned to billets	
"	25.4.15		Coys training in the morning. Sports in the afternoon	
"	26.4.15		do. do	
"	27.4.15		Orders to be prepared to move from E.Fur. onwards	
"	28.4.15		Coys training in morning. Sports in the afternoon	
"	29.4.15		do do	
"	30.4.15	4.15pm	Moved and 9th Inf Bde. by march route to the ST MOMELIN area. — Bn in huts & tents at that HALTE.	

WAR DIARY or INTELLIGENCE SUMMARY

Army Form C. 2118

Place	Date	Hour	Summary of Events and Information	Remarks and references to Appendices
	April 1915		**STRENGTH**	
			Officers OR	
			Strength at beginning of month 40 847	
			" " end " " 27 450 Lt Col L.H. Bacelli DSO MC, Major F. Sweet RE	
			Drafts received during " 2 155	
			CASUALTIES	
			Killed 3 2/Lt B.C. Peach, 2/Lt H.D'A. Champney, 2/Lt S.R. Hotton	
			Wounded 3 153 Capt. Lord, 2/Lt G.F.W. Jennings, 2/Lt S. Rott	
			" & missing 1 1F 2/Lt A.V. Deans	
			Missing 2 133 Capt A.M. Shaw, 2/Lt T. Binns	
			36 2/Lt A.R. Mather Capt. E.L. Downs	
			Evac. Sick 2 154 Capt W.D. Wilkinson DSO MC, & Indian Army	
			Other Causes 4 Lt. Col. King, Capt. Aw.T. Benfrey, 2/Lt. Col. Jowett, Lt 5th York R.	
			15 SEE	
			Remarks	
			Lieut. W.A. Wain struck off the establishment.	

J. C...
Lieut Colonel R.E.
Commdg 12th (S) Bn York. Regiment
(Tees-side Pion srs)

XV Corps   "First Army"

I wish to express my appreciation of the great bravery and endurance with which all ranks have fought and held out (during the last five days*) against overwhelming numbers. It has been necessary to call for great exertions, and more must still be asked for, but I am confident that, at this critical period when the existance of the British Empire is at stake, all ranks of the First Army will do their very best.

(Sd) H. S. Horne.
General
Commanding First Army.

First Army. H.Q.
13/4/18

* Four days. 9th - 12th April in the case of troops transferred to Second Army on 17/4/1918 from First Army)

XV Corps No. 128/14 G.
Dated 16/4/1918.

40th Division.

On your leaving the Corps the Corps Commander directs me to convey to you his appreciation of the services rendered by your Division during the operations of 9th April - April 13th.

XV Corps 16/4/18
(Sd) H Knox
Brigadier General
General Staff

40th Div. No 3/2/G.

The Division has again been engaged in heavy fighting and all Battalions have fought the enemy with great courage and determination in spite of having to face overwhelming odds. The same fighting spirit continues & I know will continue in the Division. I wish General Officers Commanding Brigades to convey to the troops under their command my sincere congratulations & thanks for their gallant behaviour under trying circumstances.

J. Ponsonby, Major General
Commanding 40th Division
19/4/18

A

Narrative of operations from 12.0 midnight 8/9th April to 12.0 midnight 14/15th April 1918.

At midnight 8/9th April 1918, the Battn was billeted as follows:- 1 Coy ("Y") + H.Q. BAC ST MAUR, 1 Coy (X) RUE DE QUESNOY, 1 Coy (W) SAILLY-SUR-LA-LYS. Transport near CROIX-DE-BACK

At 4.0 AM on 9th April the enemy opened a heavy bombardment on all billets occupied by the Battn At 6.0 am the Battn "stood to" in billets. At 11.15 am orders were received from H.Q. 40th Div for 2 Coys to occupy a line of trenches in front of BAC ST MAUR from SAILLY S. to RUE de BIACHE. At 11.30 am "X" Coy were ordered to proceed to FLUEBAIX and reinforce the Garrison there. When "X" Coy reached BALETTE FARM they got in touch with the enemy, and being heavily pressed, fought a rear guard action to the left bank of the RIVER LYS and took up a position near Pt de la BOUDRETTE, with 145 A.T. Coy R.E on left.
At 11.30 am "W" & "Y" Coys. took up the line from SAILLY S. to RUE de BIACHE. They had been in position 5 minutes when the enemy attacked in large numbers with many light Mach. guns and as these Coys had no troops on the flanks they were forced to retire. 2nd/Lt Champney + 15 men with 1 Lewis Gun covered the retirement of W Coy.

It was decided due to the artillery near in
the 2nd Bombay Bombers for now
Nor.H. Bay for supply dump. 2nd Bombay
fine the hills had turned into two light
M.y. bay often other fighting in place are
Prisoners were captured including ten up a
lookouts on the left bank of the RIVER LYS on the
left of X Day. The positions are like under
about 40 pm when the left flank of the Bath was
fired to withdraw about 1000 ams to the enemy
wooding towing the left flank.

About 60 pm a Batt of 28th Div came up with the
intention of taking CROIX de BAC, BAC ST MAUR and
SAILLY. The Batt further advances on the right
flank of the Batt with the R.R., 50th Div in support.
The Counter attack was unsuccessful

10-11-18
At 2-0 am a 10-11-18 the Bn 25th Div
Counter attacks again. W.y Coys were in
reserve at 5 y Coy were shelled to protect the
right flank. The attack was familiar
successful and the lines were pushed, but
the enemy attacks again and there our
back to our original positions on outskirts
of STEENWERCK SWITCH retaken by Rochin
(East Bn) same under orders of the Bde General R.G.
Conway. Misc Bn 119th Bde. The Bn were
withdrawn about 8 am into reserve at

PETIT MORTIÈR. About 2.0 pm a message was received from 14th H.L.I. that the enemy were attacking and this Coy moved up to reinforce the 14th H.L.I on the left of STEENWERCK SWITCH.
11-4-18.

On 11.4.18 the Battn was mixed up with the Misc Battn 119 Bde and conformed to the movements under the orders of Lt Col Brown MC when the Div was relieved.
On the night of 11/12th when the Battn was relieved by 31st Div the Battn was withdrawn from the line and concentrated near STRAZEELE

Casualties.
The following casualties occurred during these operations:-

3 Off. 28. OR Killed   4. Off 154 OR wounded
1 "   15   " wounded missing
2 "   117   " unaccounted for

                                   Lieut Colonel R.E.
                        Commdg 12th (S) Bn Yorks Regt
                             (Tees-side Pioneers)

40th Div. No 1115/22 (4)

O.C.,
   12th Yorkshire Regt (P)

The following is a copy of a letter received from the G.O.C. 50th Division.

"I shall be glad if I may express my appreciation of the excellent work done by the 12th Yorkshire Regiment (Pioneers) while attached to this Division.

After a long period in the trenches, the cheerfulness & zeal with which the Battalion has carried out any work allotted it, reflects the highest credit upon officers & men."

The Major-General Commanding directs me to say that the receipt of the letter has given him great pleasure.

The battalion under your command has always done all and more than was expected of it, under all circumstances, & he congratulates you on its efficiency.

(Signed) W. CARTER, Captain
General Staff - 40th Division

23rd Feb: 1918

12th (S.) BN.
YORKSHIRE REGT.
JUN 1 1918
(TEES-SIDE PIONEERS)
No. Y.P. 33/8

D.A.G.,
3rd Echelon

Herewith War Diary for

May. 1918.

Jos Carlisle
Lieut Colonel, R.E.
Commdg 12th (S) Bn Yorks Regiment
(Tees-side Pioneers)

WAR DIARY
or
INTELLIGENCE SUMMARY
(Erase heading not required.)

Army Form C. 2118

12th (SERVICE) BATT. YORKS. REGT.

Ref. map. Sheet 27. 1/40,000.

Vol 24

Place	Date	Hour	Summary of Events and Information	Remarks and references to Appendices
KINDER BECK	1.5.18		Battalion billeted in tents and barns near KINDER BECK	
	2.5.18		-do-	
	3.5.18		-do-	
KINDER BECK	4.5.18			
	5.5.18		Battalion broken up and formed into Battalion training staff of 10 officers and 350 O.R. situated at WATTEN at S.B.w. for base depot at CALAIS. 51 O.R. 10 officers	
	6.5.18		B.T.S. in Billets near KINDER BECK.	
	7.5.18			
	8.5.18		Moved by march route into WATTEN near ESQUELBECQ.	
	9.5.18			
ESQUELBECQ	10.5.18		B.T.S. in billets near ESQUELBECQ	
	11.5.18			
	12.5.18		Moved by march route into billets at LES CINQ RUES B.25.C.7.8	
LES CINQ RUES	13.5.18			
	16.5.18		B.T.S. in billets in LES CINQ RUES. During this period B.T.S. were employed on a butchery scheme in the area RUBROUCK. VOLKERINGHOVE. BOLLEZEELE. MILLAM.	
	17.5.18			
	to			
	31.5.18			

J.A.Corbett
Lieut Colonel R.E.
Commdg 12th (S) Bn Yorks Regiment
(Tees-side Pioneers)

12TH (S.) BN,
YORKSHIRE REGT.
JUN 7 1918
(TEES-SIDE PIONEERS)
No.

> 12TH (S.) BN.
> YORKSHIRE REGT.
> JUL 1 1918
> (TEES-SIDE PIONEERS)
> No. V.P.34/25

D.A.G.
3rd Echelon

Herewith War Diary for June, 1918.

Lieut Colonel
Commdg 12th (S) Bn Yorks Regiment
(Tees-side Pioneers)

12th (SERVICE) BATT. YORKS. REGT.

WAR DIARY or INTELLIGENCE SUMMARY

Army Form C. 2118

12 Yorkshire R
Ref Map HAZEBROUCK. 5A.
1/100000
Vol 25

Place	Date	Hour	Summary of Events and Information	Remarks and references to Appendices
LES CINQ RUES nr BORREZELLE	1.6.18 to 22.6.18		Battalion training. Staff in billets nr Les Cinq Rues (Ricksong) Lt Col H.W. BECHER D.S.O. took over command of the Battalion 3.6.18 vice Major (A/Lt Col) T.H. CARLISLE D.S.O. M.C. R.E.	
LA BELLE HOTESSE	23.6.18	9.0 am	B.T.S. moved into huts and bivouacs near LA BELLE HOTESSE	
	28.6.18		B.T.S. absorbed into establishment of 17. (S) Batt WORCESTER R. (Lt Col H.W. BECHER D.S.O. assumed command of 17 WORCESTER R. 12th (S) BATT YORK R (S) ceased to exist.	

McLure
Lieut Colonel
Commdg 12th (S) Bn Yorks Regiment
(Tees-side Pioneers)

12th Battalion Yorkshire Regiment (P).

Nominal Roll of Officers posted to 17th Bn. Worcestershire Regt.

RANK			Initials & Name	
Subs've	Temp.	acting		
Major	Lt. Col.		H. W. Becher. D.S.O.	
	Major		T. H. Carlisle. D.S.O., M.C. RE	
	"		C. M. Southey.	
	Capt.		A. C. Mildred	
	"		T. K. G. Ridley.	
			W. N. Crosby. M.C.	
			H. N. Thomas.	
	Lieut.		C. W. Hogg.	
	"		R. C. Taylor.	
	"		G. A. Dixon.	
	"		E. Mulhall.	

12th Battalion Yorkshire Regiment (P)

Nominal Roll of W.O's, P.60s and Men transferred to 17th Bn. Worcester Regt. (P)

Reg'tl No.	Rank and Name	Reg'tl No.	Rank and Name
9408	RSM Millner. W.	20814	L.C. Black. R.J.
200546	RQMS Mawer. J.C.	25068	" Scaife. J.W.
19914	CSM Armstrong. A.	20954	" Hislent. J.
19933	" Hermiston. E.P.	23941	" Smith. A.C.
19912	" Banham. T.O.	22593	Pte. Bainbridge. R.
19940	CQMS Featherstone. A.E.	46148	" Brooks. J.
19948	" Ferguson. A.	19956	" Rycroft. H.
21207	" Norman. J.	21377	" Copeland. J.
A2250	A/S/Sgt. Martin. G.	20200	" Davison. R.
20007	Sgt. Punn. W.	46628	L.C. Gray. A.
19006	" Knowles. W.	25282	Pte. McCarthy. C.
21445	" Jefferson. A.J.	21378	" Moller. G.N.
20205	" Shayne. J.	20884	" Gollock. R.
20066	" Hight. D.	22054	" Lannon. J.
22568	" Wilson. J.W.	21052	" Rutter. H.
23932	" Gillespie. W.A.	21330	" Stephenson. C.
46122	" Bruce. G.	19949	" Skitten. W.
15109	" Barney. T.	20812	" Trafford. T.
21047	Cpl. Allinson. T.W.	20972	" " J.W.
22651	" McCarthy. C.	19996	" Tate. T.
20817	" Goodrum. H.C.	20181	" Thompson. J.
19493	" Bartell. J.H.	19043	" Rodgers. C.
47928	" Wright. E.G.	34819	" Hardaker. E.

www.ingramcontent.com/pod-product-compliance
Lightning Source LLC
Chambersburg PA
CBHW081553160426
43191CB00011B/1913